GW00982541

Charles Tisdall of County Meath, 1740–51

Maynooth Studies in Local History

SERIES EDITOR Raymond Gillespie

This volume is one of five short books published in the Maynooth Studies in Local History series in 2014. Like their predecessors they range widely, both chronologically and geographically, over the local experience in the Irish past. Chronologically they span the world of the medieval priory at Fore to the labour movement in Derry at the beginning of the twentieth century and geographically from Cork to Derry and from Mayo to Meath. Socially they move from the working people of Derry through the emerging medical professionals in Cork to the landlord worlds of Charles Tisdall and the Nolans of Logboy. In doing so they demonstrate the vitality of the study of local history in Ireland and reveal the range of possibilities open to anyone interested in studying the local past. Those possibilities involve the dissection of the local experience in the complex and contested social worlds of which it is part. Such studies of local worlds over such long periods are vital for the future since they not only stretch the historical imagination but provide a longer perspective on the evolution of local societies in Ireland and help us to understand more fully the complex evolution of the Irish experience. These works do not simply chronicle events relating to an area within administrative or geographically determined boundaries, but open the possibility of understanding how and why particular regions had their own personality in the past. Such an exercise is clearly one of the most exciting challenges for the future.

Like their predecessors these five short books are reconstructions of the socially diverse worlds of the poor as well as the rich, women as well as men and reconstruct the way in which those who inhabited those worlds lived their daily lives, often little affected by the large themes that dominate the writing of national history. In addressing these issues, studies such as those presented in these short books, together with their predecessors, are at the forefront of Irish historical research and represent some of the most innovative and exciting work being undertaken in Irish history today. They also provide models that others can follow up and adapt in their own studies of the Irish past. In such ways will we understand better the regional diversity of Ireland and the social and cultural basis for that diversity. They, with their predecessors, convey the vibrancy and excitement of the world of Irish local history today.

Maynooth Studies in Local History: Number 114

Charles Tisdall of County Meath, 1740–51
from spendthrift youth to improving landlord

Marion Rogan

FOUR COURTS PRESS

Set in 10pt on 12pt Bembo by
Carrigboy Typesetting Services for
FOUR COURTS PRESS LTD
7 Malpas Street, Dublin 8, Ireland
www.fourcourtspress.ie
and in North America for
FOUR COURTS PRESS
c/o ISBS, 920 N.E. 58th Avenue, Suite 300, Portland, OR 97213

ISBN 978–1–84682–515–6

Printed in Ireland
by SprintPrint, Dublin.

Contents

Acknowledgments

I wish to acknowledge my sincere gratitude to my MA thesis supervisor, Professor Jacqueline Hill, for her expert guidance, painstaking attention to detail and the courtesy with which she directed me every step of the way. I would like to thank the History Department of NUI Maynooth, who provided support during my MA programme there, Professor Terence Dooley, Mr Rob Goodbody and Mr Denis Cronin and in particular Professor Raymond Gillespie for his good-humoured encouragement throughout and for inviting me to contribute to this series.

I owe an immense debt of gratitude to the generosity and hospitality of Anthony and Jackie Tisdall for welcoming me into their home and granting me access to the private Tisdall papers, without which, this study would not have been possible; to Sandra and Paul Hogan, Charlesfort House, for graciously allowing me entrance to their house and demesne on numerous occasions; to Éamon Courtney for photographs and to Patsy Cassidy for guiding me around Swanlinbar. I also record my appreciation to Tony Coogan for his invaluable guidance towards sources on the Tisdall family and estate. I also thank my colleagues on the MA Local History course 2010–12 for their interchange of ideas, opinions and practical support.

Thanks are also due to many libraries and institutions: Public Record Office of Northern Ireland, the National Archives of Ireland, the National Library of Ireland, Armagh Public Library, the library staff in National University of Ireland, Maynooth, the staff in Trinity College map department, Registry of Deeds, Cavan County Library and Meath County Library, in particular librarians, Tom French and Frances Tallon. Finally, and especially, I record my thanks to my husband Peter and grown-up children, Estella, Maedhbh, Ian, Clodagh, Fiona, Aileen and Peter for their support and encouragement and to whom this small book is dedicated.

I am grateful to the following for permission to use illustrations: Anthony Tisdall (figs. 2, 6, 7), Éamon Courtney (figs. 4, 12), Paul and Sandra Hogan (fig. 11) and Ordnance Survey Ireland (figs. 8, 9, 10; permit no. MP 0008213).

Introduction

This study begins in 1668 with the manor of Martry, a small Co. Meath manor straddling the banks of the river Blackwater mid-way between Navan and Kells. Martry was a place set apart. It was not Navan, not Kells, not just somewhere in between either. It had its own personality. Its unique identity continued to be cultivated and nurtured by the longevity of the Tisdall landlords who purchased the manor and managed the estate for three centuries. Sometime in the early 17th century Michael Tisdall I, the first of the family in Ireland, arrived in Castleblaney, Co. Monaghan, probably from Teesdale in northern England.[1] In the 1630s he married Anne Singleton, a member of a prominent settler family. They had seven sons and two daughters.[2] In 1668, his eldest son Michael Tisdall II leased the manor of Martry in Co. Meath, containing 1,900 acres, from Nicholas Darcy, an Irish Papist (table 1).[3]

In the Tisdall papers, dated 1668, there is a defeasance by Nicholas Darcy of Plattin to Michael Tisdall II, followed in 1669 by a fine between the two for the manor of Martry. A defeasance was a condition in a contract, the performance of which voided the contract.[4] Darcy's lands had been confiscated following the 1641 rebellion but had been partially restored by the court of claims.[5] Tisdall renewed the lease in 1669 and purchased the manor in 1672 from Darcy who appears to have been in financial difficulty.[6] In the three decades 1641–72, the estate had undergone a major shift in landownership. It became the preserve of a Protestant gentleman of English extraction. Many of the Anglo-Normans and native Irish remained but were consigned to the tenantry.[7]

Michael Tisdall II was justice of the peace in 1679. He resided mainly in Dublin. His elder son, William, inherited the estate on his father's death. During William's minority, the estate was managed by his uncle James Tisdall, later MP for Ardee in Co. Louth. William married Frances FitzGerald, sister of the 19th earl of Kildare. William's elder son, Michael III, succeeded to the manor. Michael had become MP for Ardee the previous year when his uncle James retired due to ill-health. Michael now divided his time between managing his estate in Martry and his parliamentary duties. He died aged 33 and the estate passed to his elder son, Charles, who was then only 7 years old. During Charles' minority the estate was administered by the lawyer, Charles Hamilton, Dunboyne, Co. Meath, William Waller, a neighbouring landowner, and his uncle, the Revd George Tisdall. Charles managed the estate from 1740 until he died in 1757 at the young age of 37. Most of the Tisdall landlords, except William and Charles Arthur, died very young and the estate was overseen during their minorities by a variety of

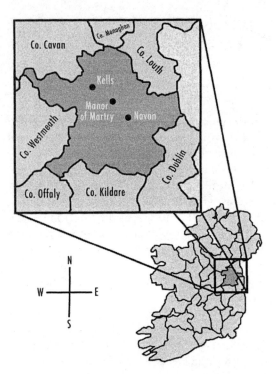

1 Co. Meath, showing location of manor of Martry.

trustees. In only one instance, when William handed the estate over to his son Michael III in 1714, did the heir take over immediately from his father. For 40 of the 122 years of the Tisdall stewardship of this estate between 1681 and 1803, the estate was administered by an amalgam of trustees, relatives and lawyers. What effect, detrimental or otherwise, did this have on the stability and economic growth of the estate? How did the estate evolve and develop during the period? These are questions this study will address.

The Tisdalls of Martry were well connected socially and politically. Though none was titled, some married into the titled class and all moved in high circles. William's brother-in-law, Robert (1675–1744), was the 19th earl of Kildare, his nephew-in-law, James (1722–73) the 20th earl, became the 1st duke of Leinster. William's father, Michael II, married Anne Barry, niece of Sir James Barry (1601–72), later the first Lord Santry (1661). Uncles, cousins, in-laws were MPs. The three Tisdalls who owned Martry in the 18th century (1714–94) did not live long enough to reach their potential. All died in their thirties. Who knows what great offices in the state they would have attained had they lived longer? Charles Tisdall (1719–57), the focus of this short book, seemed to have suffered from poor health. His account book refers to many payments to doctors, surgeons and apothecaries.[8] Tradition holds that the reason he undertook the building of a new demesne

Table 1. Tisdall landlords, 1668–1835

Landlord	Ownership dates	Year of death	Age	Relation to previous
Michael II	1668–81	1681	44	
William	1689–1714	1714*	57	Elder son
Michael III	1714–26*	1726	33	Elder son
Charles	1740–57	1757	38	Elder son
Michael IV	1776–94	794	39	Elder son
Charles Arthur	1803–35	1835	53	Eldest son

Source: Burke, Burke's *Records.*

house, which he named Charlesfort House after himself, in Athgaine Little, on higher ground and away from the rivers, was for health reasons (fig. 11).[9] Mount Tisdall, alias Bloomsbury House (fig. 3), lay at the confluence of two rivers, the Blackwater and Borora, and a heavy mist and fog still descends on the valley there in evening time, which may have posed difficulties for Charles if he had respiratory problems.

This study will concentrate on the period 1740 to 1751 on the Tisdall estate in Co. Meath. The first chapter will deal primarily with the personality of the landlord, his lifestyle and pastimes, as seen through the pages of his account book. The second chapter will focus on Charles Tisdall's stewardship of his Meath estate, 1740–51. Charles owned many properties in Drogheda in Co. Louth and in the city of Dublin, which included a brewery in Church Street; however, a consideration of these is outside the scope of this short book.[10] It will concentrate on the management structure he established on his estate in Meath, and his relationships with the tenants as observed through terms of leases, land tenure and rents. The third chapter will focus on the detailed improvements Charles Tisdall initiated and delivered on his estate, among them, the new house, Charlesfort House, the landscaped demesnes, tree plantation and the linen 'factory'. The study will conclude by examining the legacy he left to his community.

Nothing has been written on the landed estates of the Meath Blackwater region in the early 18th century except *Charlesfort: the story of a Meath estate and its people 1668–1968.*[11] *Charlesfort* tells the story of the Tisdall estate over a period of 300 years. The scope of that short book is wide and does not provide an in-depth analysis of any one period. Anthony Doyle's study of the Leslie estate at Glaslough, Co. Monaghan, was geographically closest to the Tisdall estate in Meath.[12] He dealt with estate management, the impact of external events on the community, the changes within the community and its economy 1800–41. Relevant works on the 18th century include Denis Cronin's study of Monivea in Co. Galway, a small, yet distinct, rural community in a particular place over a 64-year time-span during the 18th century.[13] W.H. Crawford's study of the Abercorn estate does likewise for north-west Ulster.[14] Joe Clarke's book on *Christopher Bellew and his Galway estates, 1763–1826* covers the same period though unusually this looks at the estate of a powerful Catholic family.[15]

Terence Dooley claims that estate papers 'reveal the reality of estate life as opposed to the myth which has often been handed down in oral history' or in biased histories.[16] This study uses this idea to unveil 11 years of Charles Tisdall's life as a Co. Meath landlord, as presented through the pages of his account book. What remains of the Tisdall estate papers can be divided into two categories; first, those accessible in the National Library of Ireland on microfilm, and second, those in private ownership, listed in the National Library of Ireland report on private collections no. 290 and the supplementary report on the Tisdall papers (from 1680), no. 426. Not all of the latter still survive. Many were lost when the family moved from Ireland to England in 1968.[17] Fortunately, some manuscripts had been partially transcribed by John Ainsworth.

Whereas few papers survive for the Tisdall estate for the first half of the 18th century, among what does is a priceless resource: Charles Tisdall's account book for the period 1740–51. It has survived the sale of the estate and the family's transfer from Ireland to England and is an intimate glimpse into the life of a young Co. Meath landlord, between the ages of 21 and 32, in the mid-18th century. Never meant for public use or examination, the book contains a wealth of engrossing detail of many aspects of Charles' life, and obversely the life of his tenants, employees, associates and friends. A hitherto-untapped reservoir of unique value, it presents an invitation that cannot be turned down, an enticement to delve deeper.[18]

A further factor, making Charles' account book worthy of closer scrutiny, is that very few comparable or as comprehensive account books for the 18th century have been discovered to date. Richard Edgeworth's personal account for 1759 to 1770 survives in the National Library of Ireland, as does a copy of the diary of John Pratt for the years 1745 to 1747.[19] The son of a squire from Agher in Co. Meath, John was a contemporary of Charles' and was a fellow member of the Meath grand jury. Twenty years earlier, and from a different social class, the land agent, Nicholas Peacock, recorded his receipts and spending.[20] This study will add another name to the list. It will include a further social class, the landed country gentleman of a relatively modest estate.

An additional dynamic, making this subject distinctive, is that Charles' stewardship of the estate began under the most dramatic and unfavourable climatic circumstances with the great frost of 1739–41, which lasted for 21 months and devastated the country, causing famine and disease. The river Boyne and its tributary, the Blackwater, which ran through the Tisdall estate, were completely frozen. Navan town held a sheep-roasting banquet on the Boyne, as did Charles Tisdall on the Blackwater. He roasted a male sheep and one side of a bullock.

'The other side [of the bullock] was boiled on the ice of the Blackwater at his [Charles'] place ... it never penetrated the bottom of the ice.'[21] This disaster was followed almost immediately by a frenzy of building and improvement from the 1740s onwards. Charles Tisdall was an early forerunner of the improving movement, building a new demesne house, planting trees and hedges, improving roads and bridges and establishing a linen factory. Lastly, although Charles was the young untitled owner of a modest estate, he lived the life of a suave, sophisticated, cultured gentleman with all the trappings of luxury expected of a much grander gentleman on a much larger estate. His new house was designed by Richard Castle and he had his portrait painted by Stephen Slaughter (1697–1765), one of the foremost portrait painters of the day.[22] His lifestyle was perhaps resonant of the lifestyle of his closest neighbour Thomas Taylor of Headfort or his relatives the earl of Kildare and Philip Tisdall, later attorney general (1760), who lived 'in a style of extraordinary magnificence'.[23] Was Charles, as Toby Barnard puts it, making 'the grand figure'?[24]

Charles Tisdall's account book is the main primary source used in this study. It is very manageable, legible and user-friendly. It is almost intact apart from some pages torn by Boswell, the family dog, in recent years.[25] It contains the financial dealings for an 11-year period in one book, with receipts on left-hand page and payments on right-hand page, a month's activity on two pages. Underlying these figures is the story and lifestyle of an 18th-century country gentleman of the landed gentry class, who led a privileged life of luxury. Indirectly, it is also a record of the lives and times of the people who populated Tisdall's life. It highlights, albeit obliquely, all that this improving young landlord achieved in the short years of his tenure and how this improvement in turn affected the social and economic life of his locality.[26] The book is supplemented by a further account book that survives, that of Robert Waller, the estate agent on the Tisdall estate during Charles' minority, 1727 to 1740, and sets the backdrop for this study.[27] A limited collection of Tisdall papers preserved on microfilm in the National Library of Ireland provides further information. Particularly interesting and informative are the memoirs of 98-year-old Christie Ward who spent all his long life working on the Tisdall estate. Christie was born in 1743.[28] His story adds fascinating detail, colour and reality to the story of this community's life. A rent roll and list of securities of Michael Tisdall, relating to his property c.1792, deals with land tenure, leases and rent on the estate and gives the tenant's name, date and length of lease, acreage and location of the holding.[29] Though beyond the time limit for this work, it is a useful resource for comparing the pattern of land tenure and highlights the effects of long leases on subletting and subdivision. A document containing instruction on how to prepare flax is perhaps the first indication of the commencement of the fledgling domestic linen industry on the estate. It also contributes towards our knowledge of this estate's management.[30]

K.H. Connell holds that 'few features that distinguish the social life of Ireland in the 18th and early 19th century did not depend on the elasticity of rent.'[31] Gross rent from property and agricultural land was a major source of Tisdall's income and so is recorded in his account book. This income was supplemented by interest from debentures for the Navan–Kells turnpike road and rentals from his houses in Drogheda and in Dublin.[32] Martry parish was the centre of local government for the area under study. It was the religious and civil unit and its decisions affected the lives of the majority of people in the area under study. A transcript of the religious census of 1766 is available for the parish of Martry and two adjacent parishes of Ardbraccan and Liscarton.[33] This census records the head of the family and number of families belonging to each religious denomination, not available elsewhere for the period. When used with church records it gives a fuller religious profile of the area. The 1821 census returns survive for a number of townlands in the barony of Navan Lower including the townlands of Martry on the Tisdall estate and a microfilm copy is available in Meath County Library, Navan.[34] Although its date is 70 years outside the limit of this study, nevertheless invaluable information can be gleaned from its pages. It provides an important insight into household economy at the time. The occupation of wives is recorded in many instances in Martry. They were generally flax spinners and house servants. The numbers of flax spinners and linen weavers recorded bears testament to Charles Tisdall's legacy of establishing a domestic linen industry on his estate in 1743.[35] Spinning wheel premium records substantiate this. Several of the households are returned as having weavers, even more frequently flax spinners, living in them.[36]

Charles Tisdall changed the look of the landscape in the Meath Blackwater valley. This appearance still dominates to this day with the riparian wooded demesne of Bloomsbury House, alias Mount Tisdall, complete with its boathouse, and the Richard Castle-designed large grey mansion, Charlesfort House, the house Charles built but never lived in. They are testament to the work of this improving landlord.[37] Local place names reflect the Tisdalls' lives and work here. Castle Hill recalls the castle on the manor of Martry and the origins of this estate. 'The factory field' and 'the mill-race field' bear witness to Charles Tisdall's endeavours in the age of improvement to advance the linen industry and improve the economy of his estate.

1. The material world of Charles Tisdall

If 18th-century gentlemen kept full accounts or diaries of their receipts and spending, then very few are extant. While in Limerick Nicholas Peacock recorded the routine existence of a rural agent and modest farmer 'higher than the commonality' but outside the gentry, Charles Tisdall revealed another facet of life in mid-18th century Ireland.[1] This was the world of luxury enjoyed by a fashionable country gentleman, with its merry-go-round of travel, finery, entertainment, commodities and consumption. Apart from the arid record of receipts and payments, Charles' account book also contains occasional diary-like observations and musings, providing an intimate and fascinating insight into his world.

Charles socialized among the highest echelons of the privileged, titled and landed classes, yet he, himself, was a country gentleman of modest means on a modest estate in Co. Meath. Was he 'making the grand figure'?[2] Was he perhaps 'keeping up with the Jones' and indulging in the lifestyle of his wealthier and more influential relatives, James FitzGerald, Lord Offaly (1722–73), later 1st duke of Leinster, or his cousin Philip Tisdall (1703–77), who became attorney general in 1760.[3] Perhaps it was his neighbour, Thomas Taylor, owner of an estate of 21,000 acres whom he was emulating? The apparent contradiction between his relatively modest inheritance and his grand lifestyle is another factor that makes this study worthwhile.

The compass of this chapter is necessarily limited and will focus on the main aspects of Charles Tisdall's material world. Even so, this range is diverse. It includes Charles' passion for travel and his acquisition of fine clothes and conspicuous commodities on his sojourns abroad. It explores his leisure pursuits and the clubs and societies he patronized, the social milieu in which he mingled and his interest in music and books. It notes the furnishings and prints with which he adorned his house, and reflects on this 18th-century gentleman's apparent lavish hospitality as indicated by his expenditure on alcohol.

Charles kept meticulous financial accounts for the years 1740–51. For the purposes of this study, his stewardship may be roughly divided into two periods, 1740–6 and 1746–51, reflecting the two very different stages in his life as a country gentleman.[4] There is a seemingly contrasting, even conflicting, duality to Charles' period as landlord of a country estate. The early years were largely spent in the accumulation of commodities and consumption, the later years more devoted to improving his estate. The extravagance and lavishness of Charles' early years contrasted sharply with the poor economic state of the country between 1740

Creditor

	£	s	d
ram to Mr George Adams	2	0	1
thirty six cullen ewes to Sam. Gerrard	19	10	1½
James Savill proctor to Mr David Roberts for the last four years small tyth of the part of Mounttisdall in Donaghpatrick parish	2	5	6
for a hogshead of claret to Metge of Navan	19	0	0
for four dozen of claret to Do	3	12	0
to ... Smyth for the two last years small tyth of part of Mounttisdall in Kells parish, at the same time he agreed I should have it at twenty shillings yearly till one of us should declare off	2	0	0
for fifty ewes bought at Kells fair	18	13	3
for a WestMeath ram to Sam. Gerrard	1	2	9
to Bell for a small cart without wheels	1	10	0
to my sister in full for her allowance to ye first of last September	15	0	0
for the frete of my post chaise from Rotterdam	10	10	0
duty for do at the custom house	1	14	9½
to Mr Lennox to discharge Mr Selvin's draft on me for transporting the chaise from Rouen to Rotterdam	19	5	0
to Vareilles in full for timber & boards	5	18	2
to Gleditanes in full for wines & syder	12	3	7½
to Franks coachmaker for repairs &c. in full	7	19	5
to Gogher for a bull calf	0	16	6
to Metge for four dozen of wine & bottles	4	0	8
expences abroad	3	16	0
workmen's wages	46	15	5
domesticks wages	1	2	9
house expences including the ironmongers	22	16	0
filth & groceries	17	3	6
durables			
total	239	3	6½
by ballance resteth cash	423	8	4½
	662	11	11

2 Page from Charles Tisdall's account book, Oct. 1744.

and 1746, while his more abstemious, prudent, 'improving' phase was acted out against the backdrop of an upswing of economic growth between 1747 and 1751. The change from one phase to the other was gradual, almost imperceptible, which only a close scrutiny of his financial dealings unveils. The pendulum swung gradually from a constant whirlwind of travel and personal spending to house building, tree plantation and improving the estate. An examination of his early, more profligate years is more enlightening with regard to his material possessions. Charles' lifestyle is acted out against the historical context of the mid-18th century, beginning during the disastrous climatic conditions of the early 1740s and the resulting poor crops, poverty, famine and disease.[5] It ends in the early 1750s with the commencement of an upward curve of improved rentals from land and Dublin properties, incomes which supported Charles.[6]

Charles Tisdall (1719–57) was born at Mount Tisdall, near Kells in Co. Meath, the family seat since 1668. He was the elder son of Michael Tisdall III, MP for Ardee, 1713 and 1715, and Catherine Palmer. Catherine was the daughter of Right Honourable William Palmer, principal secretary in Ireland, secretary for war and commissioner for appeals.[7] William Palmer was also MP for Kildare in 1695 and Castlebar in 1723. Michael Tisdall III died in 1727, when Charles was a 7-year-old boy. In his will, 25 January 1724/5 and proved 12 February 1727/8, he appointed the Honourable Joshua Allen, Colonel Sandford Esq. and Charles Campbell Esq. as guardians to his children.[8] Some years later, Catherine married the Revd Dr Edward Hudson. Charles lived with them in Henry Street in Dublin, until he was 13, when he passed into the care of his guardians, under the conditions of his father's will. Educated privately by the Revd Dr Hudson and later Dr St Paul, Charles entered Trinity College, Dublin, graduating in 1738 with a BA degree.[9] While a student, he lived in Trinity College and one of his first recorded payments in February 1740/1 was for £65 paid to William Napper, Loughcrew, Co. Meath, for a room that he 'bought in the college in full'.[10] An entry in his account book the following January refers to the £25 15s. 6d. 'costs of a suit in chancery commenced by William Napper Esq. against Mr Hudson as my tutor about my room in the college'.[11] For the 13 years, 1727–40, following Michael III's death, the Tisdall estate was in a state of limbo, managed by executors, Charles Hamilton and William Waller, a neighbouring landlord from Allenstown, with Robert Waller, William's relative, acting as agent.[12] The demesne lands at Mount Tisdall were set to Constantine Maguire, Mrs Delamere and to John Lowther at various times from 1730 until Charles took over the demesne in 1740.[13] A young inexperienced man with no father's guiding hand to direct him, unfamiliar with the estate, having spent all his youth away from it in Dublin with his mother and the Revd Dr Hudson, later in Trinity College, Dublin, Charles came from the sheltered, cosseted life of academia and the Grand Tour to manage his Meath estate.

Charles' early years were a merry-go-round of spending on travel, fine clothes, personal accessories and the trappings of a country gentleman. Much of his time

3 Mount Tisdall, alias Bloomsbury House, Co. Meath.

and resources were expended in the pursuit of pleasure, in travelling, attending balls, races, spas and card playing. Whether the spate of spending was due to the novelty of the newly accessed inheritance or the extravagance of youth is uncertain. More likely it was a continuation of the lifestyle he had enjoyed in the carefree period following his graduation from Trinity College in 1738 and prior to his coming of age in October 1740. On 9 July 1738, the land agent Robert Waller paid £1,000 into Charles' account on direction of his guardian, Robert Sandford, very probably to finance his Grand Tour, an essential core element of a young gentleman's education in the 18th century.[14] Charles spent September, October and November 1739 in Turin in Italy, not returning to Ireland until 12 April 1740.[15]

He continued to travel extensively in Europe after attaining his majority. There is no mention of his being caught up in any of the wars ongoing in Europe in the 1740s. He visited Rome and Leghorn in Italy, Paris and Rouen in France as well as England. His travels in Ireland were equally extensive, to Dublin, to Swanlinbar in Co. Cavan for the spa, to Omagh in Co. Tyrone and to Rathfriland in Co. Down.[16] In an abstract of his end-of-year expenses in 1744, he ruefully regrets the money 'spent abroad, all of which might be saved if I stay'd constantly in the country'. Perhaps his musing hints at the beginnings of a change of mindset and marks the transition from the early spendthrift days to the 'improving' landlord phase. The £179 5s. that he expended that year on 'expenses abroad', represented almost 28 per cent of his income and exceeded by 8 per cent the combined income generated from rent and miscellaneous sources for the year.[17] Travel was a far from comfortable pursuit in 18th-century Ireland. Roads were bad and travel was slow. In 1729 Dean Swift, an inveterate traveller, who frequented the spa in Swanlinbar, complained that 'generally speaking all over the kingdom the roads are deplorable'.[18] Charles undertook the first of such tours to the north of Ireland from May to August 1741. He was in Rathfriland in Co. Down on 28 May, where he left 9s. 9d. with the local people, to drink 'the night the news of Admiral Vernon's success at Carthagena'.[19] Drinking toasts to victories in battle was a common ritual among the gentry at the time. On 25 April 1746 Charles celebrated 'the duke's victory in Scotland', probably the duke of Cumberland's victory at the battle of Culloden, with a barrel of ale costing £1 2s. 9d.[20]

He records that 'diet and lodging at Mourn' and expenses on 'the way home' amounted to £13 4s. 2d. He spent August 1741 in Omagh and Enniskillen in Co. Fermanagh and in Swanlinbar in Co. Cavan, this trip cost £16 9s. 9d. His step-father, the Revd Dr Edward Hudson, was from Omagh, so this is possibly why Charles visited there so regularly. He also mentions being in Omagh again in October 1746.[21] The months of July and August were high season in Swanlinbar, a well-renowned spa in the 18th century favoured by gentry and peasant alike. Thomas Taylor writing to his father, Sir Thomas Taylor, Kells, from The Hague in Holland in July 1741, expressed the hope that 'you will not miss drinking the swaddling bar waters, as this is charming weather for them'.[22] Charles went to Swanlinbar on alternate years. The town had lodging-houses to let to wealthy patrons in the season, with space for their servants to sustain comfortable living, although Richard Twiss claimed later in 1776 that the accommodation was very indifferent.[23] Isaac Butler, who toured there in 1744, claimed that almost every house 'has for sale Aquavitae or whiskey – a wholesome balsamic diuretic'.[24] Charles spent a fortnight in Maon's establishment there in July 1741, 'taking the waters'. He may have found the accommodation in Maon's less than satisfactory that summer, since on 21 August he and six of his gentleman friends organized a whip-round for a Mr Cross, 'to encourage his having accommodation for lodgers' the following year.[25] Each contributed a non-refundable deposit of a moydore, a Portuguese gold coin current in England in the early 18th century and valued by Charles at £1 9s. 3d.

The waters of the well had a high sulphur and iron content. Dr John Rutty MD (1698–1775), an eminent Dublin physician, visited the spa in 1739. He conducted a number of experiments on its waters and cited several instances of their curative powers especially for stomach problems, when taken internally, as well as 'rebellious diseases of the skin', when applied externally. They had a palliative effect on coughs. The waters were reputed to be a great cure for a hangover and Dr Rutty cites a gentleman who affirmed that two or three quarts of the water taken, 'quite sobered him after a night spent drinking claret'. Some of Dr Rutty's patients had previously visited the spa in Bath in England in vain looking for a cure.[26] However, a number of weeks spent in Swanlinbar drinking the waters, produced results. The waters could also be bottled, corked and sent to other destinations. Charles used this facility in 1743, when there is no record of his visit to the spa, but he still availed of its restorative waters by getting 'four dozen of spa water' delivered at a cost of 5s. 5d. Charles lodged with Mrs Cross for three weeks in 1745, so the whip-round of four years' previously must have had the desired effect. His expenses amounted to £11 7s. 6d. At the end of his vacation, he gave Mrs Cross a donation of £3 8s. 3d. towards the cost of making a road from the town to the spa, no doubt to facilitate his easier access to it. The spa was situated less than a mile from the town. Both Charles and his sister, Catherine, may have benefitted from the new road when, along with their servant, they spent eight weeks in Mrs Cross's establishment in the summer of 1747. Charles used three horses for the journey. Lodgings and diet for himself, his sister and a servant, along with grass for the horses, cost £13 6s. for the duration.[27] 'Taking the waters' did not occupy all Charles' time and energy. He attended a ball there on 12 August 1741 and the price of the ball, together with the claret he consumed, set him back £4 11s.[28]

Whether Charles' visits to Swanlinbar spa were solely for health reasons is not clear. He died at the age of 37 and seems to have suffered from poor health on several occasions throughout his life, perhaps resulting from a serious illness when he was 7 years old. In May 1727, the estate agent, Robert Waller, recorded settling an outstanding bill for £21 15s. 1d. with the surgeon, Mr Forthry, and an apothecary for caring for Charles when he was 'dangerously ill and lame'.[29] He was ill again in January 1744/5 during a period of heavy snow and paid the substantial sum of £17 1s. 3d. to a physician, for 'taking care of me in my illness the whole time'.[30] There are references to payments to other doctors too and numerous payments to George Cripps, an apothecary in Kells.[31] But since visiting spas was a fashionable pursuit with the gentry, a combination of both reasons is the more likely. Swanlinbar was approximately 50 miles from Mount Tisdall on the coach road from Kells to Enniskillen. Charles didn't need to avail of the existing post chase. He had a new landau, costing £80, purchased in 1741, which made travelling more comfortable.[32] Four years later, while in Paris, he purchased a 'French post chaise'.[33] He paid Mr Lennox £6 6s. to convey it from Paris to Rouen and a further £19 5s. to transport it from Rouen to Rotterdam. He fitted it with crimson curtains, lamps and a new harness for the horses in 1745/6.[34] He must have looked every inch the dashing figure of a landed gentleman in his French post-chaise with its crimson curtains, travelling to and from the spa in Swanlinbar. Despite the acquisition of the post-chaise, Charles still kept his landau and had it restored in November 1745. Purchasing a new set of wheels, cleaning and painting it cost him £9 10s. 3d.[35]

No sooner had Charles returned from Swanlinbar in 1741, than he was off again travelling, this time to England and the Continent, for the three months of September, October and November. He travelled to Leghorn (Livorna) via London, stopping off there to borrow £400 at 6 per cent interest from Messrs Knox & Craghead, bankers in London, at the direction of Mr Albert Gladstone, to finance his Grand Tour. This loan represented almost 20 times his cash

4 Brass button from jacket of servant's livery.

reserves.[36] Charles returned briefly from the Continent to London on 1 October, when he paid Mr Hill, hop merchant in Thames Street, London, for the freight cost of two trunks from Leghorn and expenses at the Custom House.[37] He returned to France and spent October abroad on a spending spree in Paris.

A scrutiny of Charles' purchases reveals some eccentricities. The Tisdall coat of arms and crest were immensely important to him. *Tutantur tela coronam* 'weapons guard a crown' was assigned to his great-grandfather, Michael Tisdall II, Esq., JP, Meath, and his brothers in 1679.[38] Charles had the crest emblazoned on all manner of his possessions from a damask table cloth and napkins purchased in Drogheda, to the brass buttons on the jackets of his male servants' livery (fig. 4).[39] He ordered six dozen of these buttons from England in 1742 costing £8 8s. 4d.[40] A bloodstone that once stood in front of Charlesfort House also had his coat of arms imprinted on it.[41] On 17 July 1745, Charles paid Mr Brooks of Dublin 18s. 3d. for a copper plate of his arms; a further 100 impressions cost 2s. 2½d.

Charles' account book, especially in the early years, abounds with details of the money he spent on his dress and gives a rare insight into what a young sophisticated country gentleman wore. If clothes maketh the man, then Charles Tisdall must have appeared a handsome figure. He bought a lot of finery in Paris in 1741, displaying to the world his fine taste, extensive travel and consequently his gentility. Toby Barnard contends that dress was clearly associated with social position.[42] 'Raiment, whether wig, coat or linen indicated both rank and means'. A very detailed list of Charles Tisdall's purchases is documented for September and October 1741, less than a year after coming in to his inheritance. They ranged over a broad array of material acquisitions and luxury goods. In September, he bought a black velvet cap 'of the best quality' cambric, ribbon, and muslin for cravats and four fans.[43] On 1 October, he was in Paris where gold featured heavily in his purchases. He bought a gold headed cane for £5 13s. 9d. and a gold French horn with a seal to it. The most expensive item was a gold repeating watch for

£20 9s. 6d. He also purchased an amber egg tipped with gold. Black silk stockings, white silk stockings and material for breeches were also among his purchases.[44] By November he was in England. Here he bought more gold items, but he also bought a garnet ring for the breast of his shirt, a woman's hat and two dozen Scotch handkerchiefs.[45] In addition, he spent the further substantial amount of £62 4s. 10d. 'of which he kept no account'.[46]

In Dublin his clothes were made for him by James Hassard, Skinner Row.[47] The rents from two of his houses in Dublin were not cash transactions in the 1740s. Christopher Lynch rented Charles Tisdall's house in Cook Street, Dublin, but made breeches and gloves, costing £19, for Charles in lieu of rent.[48] Philip Reilly, another tailor, rented Charles' property in Michael's Lane, Dublin. He paid part of his rent in kind, as did his widow after his death. A year-and-a-half's rent for £10 was settled through her tailoring work.[49] On 2 November 1745, Charles paid £7 10s. for a gold fringe for a waistcoat weighing 12½ ounces.[50] Less than three weeks later, he bought silver lace and buttons for a suit of clothes costing £11 4s. 7½d. In January, he bought linen and cambric to make shirts.[51]

He was particularly meticulous in his account keeping in the early days. Later on, he appears to have purchased less or ceased enumerating every article of clothing. Perhaps he didn't need any more finery, only the basics, having well stocked up in the early years. From January 1743/4, the items 'durables' and 'apparel' appeared monthly under expenditure. Individual items of clothing, if bought, were not recorded. His Dublin tenant, Christopher Lynch continued to supply him with breeches and gloves.[52] Charles included his 'regimental accoutrements' with durables and apparel in April 1744.[53] What they consisted of is not mentioned. Only the words, 'regimental accoutrements', hint at Charles' involvement in a local militia, a Protestant civilian auxiliary defence force raised whenever the government of the day perceived itself under threat from foreign invasion and disbanded when the crisis was over. The militia was raised in 1745 in response to a feared Jacobean uprising and in the Co. Louth array that year, five of Charles' kinsmen were commissioned and mustered in the regiment of dragoons in the baronies of Louth and Ferrard.[54] Nicholas Peacock took part in an array in November 1745.[55] Fragmentary disparate pieces of evidence indicate that there was also an array in Co. Meath. It seems that John Pratt from Agher was commissioned, since he writes that he 'wore his regimentals' to an assembly in Dublin on the evening of 1 February 1745/6, having settled his bill for his 'regimentals' earlier in the day. Socializing and conviviality went hand in glove with militia life. On 4 November 1745, John Pratt dined at an inn in Summerhill in Co. Meath with Captain Roger Jones and his troops, on which occasion he 'drank to be sick'.[56] On 14 November 1745, Thomas Taylor, Lord Headfort, Kells, was commissioned as captain of a unit of infantry, probably for the town of Kells.[57]

A trawl through Charles' account book unveils no reference to his being involved in any array or parade during the period. Why he purchased regimental accoutrements a year and a half before the array in 1745 is not clear. Perhaps it was the reports of an intended French invasion of Ireland or England in February 1744 that precipitated the purchase. Perhaps sartorial vanity and ostentation played a part too, and Charles, who loved finery, was anxious to have his 'regimental accoutrements' as early as possible. By 1756, Charles was captain of one of the 12 independent troops of dragoons in Co. Meath. Two of his largest tenants, Hugh Lowther and Charles Pleasants, were cornets in his unit. His troop would have consisted of privates between the ages of 16 and 60.[58]

'Membership of voluntary boards was an indicator of social placement' and a further indicator of lifestyle, where the gentry met and mingled with their social equals and peers.[59] Charles was a member of at least three associations in 1741.[60] Attending horse races and sponsoring prizes were usual pursuits of the gentry.[61] In June, Charles paid a subscription of £5 2s. 11d. to County Down Horse Breeders' Association, and in December of that year, he sponsored a gold medal for a race, costing £2 5s. 6d.[62] Meath's proximity to Dublin ensured a busier social scene than in many other more remote rural estates. Charles subscribed to two Meath race meetings. In April 1741, August 1744 and again in September 1749, he paid £1 2s 9d. for races at Trim in Co. Meath. *Cheny's Calendar*, 1741, listed both Downpatrick and Trim as venues for races in 1741.[63] On 15 August 1744, Mr La Rüe, who appears to have been Charles' personal servant, purchased six pairs of worked ruffles for him, costing £3, perhaps in anticipation of Charles' attendance at Trim races and the ensuing expected socializing and entertaining. Charles attended the post-race ball there at the latter date, which cost 11s. 4½d. He also patronized Ratoath races in Co. Meath in 1741. Ratoath is close to Dublin and would have attracted the gentry of the city, as well as the Meath gentry. He attended a ball and supper in his club in Crow Street in Dublin on 6 December 1742, which set him back £2 19s. 7d.[64] Attendance at the assizes in Trim afforded Charles further opportunity to fraternize with other Protestant gentry after the work of managing the county affairs was finished. He drank, played cards and secured lucrative road contracts through contacts made there.

Gambling on card games was part and parcel of social occasions in the 18th century.[65] Charles enjoyed playing cards. He won £5 1s. 2d. playing whist on 2 March 1740/1.[66] 'The Goat's Whey' seems to have been a favourite haunt of his and his stay there in June 1741 cost him £7 15s. 7½d.[67] It was a profitable stay, however, for he records winning the substantial amount of £92 14s. 3d. 'at several games this month' there. Nevertheless, it didn't compensate for his greater loss of £97 16s. 11½d. while playing cards at Trim two months previously in April 1741.[68] This was probably while Charles was staying there for the Lent assizes, for on 12 April, he records £4 4s. for 'expenses at the assizes of Trim'. Another card-playing location was the Waller home in Allenstown. Charles liked to wager on other things too. In November 1743 he laid a bet of £10 with his cousin Lord Offaly, later duke of Leinster (1722–73), 'for which he is to pay me twenty guineas next May if he is not marry'd before that time'. Charles won the bet. Lord Offaly did not marry until 1746.[69]

The Irish gentry in the mid-18th century were particularly fond of outdoor activities. They liked to boat and fish.[70] It is likely that Charles enjoyed both pastimes, since the rivers Blackwater and Borora flowed past his house at Mount Tisdall and among his purchases was a trout-casting net in October 1741. In June 1744, Charles had his boat painted for £1 2s. 9d.[71] Mount Tisdall boasted a beautiful two-storey octagonal building in a prime location overlooking the confluence of the two rivers with a boathouse below and a temple above (fig. 5). The boathouse was at river level during Charles' lifetime.[72] The temple room, 14 feet in diameter, would have been a perfect setting to indulge the 18th-century passion for outdoor dining. In August 1744, Charles adorned it with an urn of Ardbraccan stone costing £3 16s. He purchased four large garden chairs in 1746.[73]

In July 1742, Charles bought a boat from Mr Taylor, Kells, which cost the large sum of £30 11s. In September 1746, he bought a 'Norway' boat from the same gentleman for £2 4s., and put an awning of sail cloth on one of his boats in November 1746.[74] On 24 April 1750, he paid £4 2s. 8½d. for 'whitening and painting the summer house and boat', no doubt in preparation for entertaining guests at the wedding of his sister Catherine to Arthur Hamilton Maxwell the following month at Mount Tisdall. He stocked the rivers with 40 brace of crayfish from Birr in Co. Offaly costing £1 2s. 9d. in June 1751 and by September, a pair of swans graced the rivers.[75] Hunting and shooting were popular pastimes among the gentry. Charles appeared to love his dogs and horses and had pet names for all of them. He purchased a hound called 'Ratler' in February 1741 for £1 9s.1d. Later in November that year, while on the Grand Tour, he bought a French Barbet hunting bitch, 'Countess', for retrieving shot wild water fowl on the rivers on his estate for 11s. 4½d. In 1749, he acquired a five-year-old bay horse, 'Tortoise' which cost him £25.[76] He owned several horses, both coach horses and cart horses, and had stables at Mount Tisdall. He also rented stables in Dublin.[77] He purchased six coach mares in Northampton in England for £81 5s. in September 1741. He bought a bay gelding in December 1744 and an English long whip the previous September.[78] Hunting and shooting required luxury accessories too, and the proper gentlemanly look extended to this aspect of Charles' life.[79] A fowling piece was acquired for £6 16s. 6d., together with a short bullet gun with swivels for £3 5s., and a new fashion shot bag.[80] He also subscribed to a 'tenis court' in 1747.[81]

The young Charles, having spent 18 years in Dublin, must have been very much a city gentleman too. Dublin was the second city of the British empire at the time and, when parliament was in session, the city was especially buzzing. Music was perceived as an 'elegant entertainment'.[82] Charles enjoyed music and the second entry in his accounts book is for a subscription to a musical academy of £3 0s. 3d.[83] He may have played a musical instrument, perhaps the flute like his brother Michael.[84] Concert-going was a fashionable pursuit rather than a display of enthusiasm for music at the time, however, and it was usual for patrons to chat or play cards during performances. In May 1741, Charles paid £3 8s. 3d. to the Philharmonic Society.[85] He was a member of 'The Bull's Head' club,

5 Boathouse on
Mount Tisdall.

Fishamble Street, Dublin, for which he paid a subscription of 11s. 4½d. in
December 1741.[86] Charles attended a concert in Aungier Street Playhouse in
December 1740. Concerts were staged regularly in Dublin as fund-raisers for
charitable causes. John Pratt of Agher attended four plays and two musical
concerts in the winter of 1745/6.[87] *Faulkner's Dublin Journal* contains advertise-
ments for seven such productions in January 1741/2. Charles spent from 13 until
29 of January 1741/2 in Dublin at a cost of £14 4s. 10d., so he may have attended
some of the performances. Perhaps on 13 January he attended the new 'Musick-
Hall' in Fishamble Street, when the duke and duchess of Devonshire hosted the
second night of 'Handel's Musical Entertainment'; admission a 'British sixpence'.[88]

One of the most famous musical events in Ireland took place in Dublin in
April 1742, when the first performance of 'Messiah' was directed by its composer
George Frederick Handel (1685–1759).[89] This premiere was the culmination of
two series of subscription concerts which had begun in December 1741. Charles
paid a subscription to Handel's first oratorios in 1741/2. The following year, he
paid a subscription of £5 13s. 9d. on 13 January 1742/3 to Mr Maxwell for Handel's
six first oratorios. In February, he spent a further £1 17s. 1d. on a 'third of Handel's
six oratorios'. In November, he paid £3 8s. 3d. for 'Arne's four concerts'. Dr
Thomas (1740–86) and Mrs Arne gave several concerts in Fishamble Street in the
winter of 1742/3.[90] Charles was also a member of a club in Crowe Street, where

attendance at a ball and supper in December 1741 cost £2 19s. 7d.[91] Music featured heavily again when his sister, Catherine, had her wedding reception in Mount Tisdall in April 1750. Charles engaged two musicians from Dublin to play there for three weeks at a cost of £3 8s. 3d.[92]

It is interesting that Charles listed books as number one on his list of necessary acquisitions in January 1740/1, 'for necessarys viz., books'.[93] Dublin and London newspapers were delivered by post to country towns from the end of the 17th century.[94] On 23 December 1744 and again on 24 February 1744/5, Charles paid Edward Martin £1 2s. 9d. for a year's supply of newspapers, thus keeping in touch with what was happening in the wider world outside Meath, Dublin and Ireland.[95] From the beginning of the 18th century, those living in Dublin could access the city's many bookshops and booksellers. Charles purchased books from many of them, including Faulkner and Moore, with whom he settled an account for £2 1s. 8½d. in December 1741.[96] Graduates of Trinity College, like Charles, could access the college library and gentlemen had a right of entry to Marsh's Library, which was established in 1707.

His literary tastes were wide and varied. Apart from books on architecture purchased in September 1742, when he decided to embark on building a new house, he also bought *An essay on the agreement between the works of the Roman poets and the remains of the ancient sculptors and painters* by Joseph Spence.[97] This may have guided him when buying statuary for his demesne later on in 1747.[98] In February 1742/3, he paid a subscription of £4 11s. for eight volumes of the *Universal history*.[99] Charles bought four volumes of a French dictionary in February 1740/1 as a present for his former tutor, Dr St Paul, costing £4 and three further volumes in March for £3 for himself, essential, no doubt, for his many trips to France.[100] In 1751, he was still adding to his library when he purchased 16 books from Mrs Hills for £2 3s. 2d.[101]

Charles may have entertained a lot and been a hospitable host. His cousin, Philip Tisdall, Stillorgan Park, known for his lavish hospitality, was reputed to have been an 'eight bottle man'.[102] Expenditure on drink featured heavily in Charles' accounts, too, in the years 1740–6, particularly in 1744. One Metges in Navan, Co. Meath, winner of a £5 premium for the best mead at the Dublin Society in 1744 to 1745, supplied drink to Mount Tisdall, while Albert Gledstone, a wine merchant in Abbey Street and Christopher Harrison in Mary's Abbey, provided it for his Dublin residence.[103] Between June and October 1744, Charles spent £94 18s. 10½d. on wines, ciders and several hogsheads of claret.[104] His reserves of cash were particularly low in October 1744, a month before the November gale rent fell due, and on 17 October, he needed to borrow £300 at 5 per cent from William Sandford.[105] Nevertheless, this didn't prevent him spending extravagantly on drink. In October alone, 16 per cent of his expenditure was on alcohol, representing 84 per cent of his income.[106] Charles' 25th birthday fell on 29 October, so perhaps he was hosting celebrations. Wine was sometimes used as currency for paying rent on the Tisdall estate. Mr Read, one of his tenants

Table 1.1. Silver purchased by Charles Tisdall

Date	Silver item	Cost	Place	Silversmith
7 Dec. 1741	Cream pot	£1 16s. 0d.	England	Not stated
28 Jan. 1741/2	6 tea spoons Strainer	£1 6s. 5½d.	Not stated	Not stated
3 May 1742	Plate stand	£8 3s. 0d.	Dublin	John Letablere
28 May 1743	Watch	£3 10s. 0d.	Not stated	Not stated
6 July 1745	Pepper box	£0 17s. 6d.	Not stated	Not stated
4 Oct. 1745	Dish for apple pyes with arms engraved	£13 4s. 5d.	Not stated	Not stated
19 Sept. 1747	Tankard, 3 casters	£16 5s. 2½d.	Not stated	Not stated
16 Apr. 1750	2 pairs candlesticks	£23 14s. 0d.	Dublin	John Letablere
18 June 1750	Silver nutmeg grater	£0 11s. 4½d.	Dublin	John Letablere
	Diamond pencil set in silver	£0 6s. 8d.	Dublin	John Letablere
	Total	**£68 14s. 7½d.**		

Source: CTAB

in Cow Lane and Church Street, Dublin, paid his £27 rent bill in April 1746 in wine and hops.[107] As the years progressed, Charles' expenditure on alcohol, as on travel, finery and card-playing, decreased.

It can reasonably be assumed that Mount Tisdall was in less than a pristine and fashionable condition when Charles returned there in 1740. It had not been lived in by the family since his father's death. Even during his lifetime, Michael III, had spent little time there, dividing his time between his estate and his parliamentary duties in Dublin. Charles' account book gives some idea of décor and prevailing fashions in a gentleman's house in the mid-18th century. One of his first purchases was purely functional and mundane, a 'bathing tub bought in Dublin'. Utensils for the house alone cost the large sum of £8 9s. 8d. on 30 May 1742.[108] In January 1741/2, he spent £3 0s. 1½d. on furniture 'for my house in the country'.[109] On 1 October, when in Paris, he bought four dozen hafts [handles] of knives and forks. In November, he got blades set and put in the hafts when he was in England.[110] Charles had an account with Mr Henry Perrot in Paris and ordered a suite of furniture 'red velvit embroidered with gold' costing £91 4s.[111] The following February, he had a parcel of earthenware sent from Rouen costing him £5 10s. 6d.[112] Charles recorded eight purchases of table silver, totalling £68 14s. 7½d. (table 1.1).[113] On three instances, he purchased the goods from John Letablere.[114] Perhaps this silverware was among the plate that, in October 1783, his son, Michael IV, had Christie Ward and his brother 'bury in the bullock yard in a heap of manure' the night before Michael set out for England. Christie recalled that 'the plate was wrapped in flannel and then in linen and put into a trunk and that again into a rough chest'.[115] Charles also bought gold items in

6 Portrait of Charles
Tisdall by Stephen
Slaughter.
Notes on back of
portrait read 'the
portrait was cleaned,
following being
covered with smoke
from a paraffin fire, by
Patrick O'Connor,
Dublin in April 1763',
'portrait was stored (at
Miller & Beatty) for
safe-keeping during the
troubles 1919–22'.

Dublin from Robert Calderwood.[116] Both John Letablere and Robert Calderwood also supplied Viceroy Hartington and the earl of Kildare.[117]

The most important room in Mount Tisdall was the 'big parlour'. This is where Charles would have received guests and entertained. In 1743/4 he spent £18 4s. 6d. on its refurbishment. He had the wainscot refitted in February 1743/4.[118] An early purchase for the parlour on 3 July 1743 was a looking glass costing £2 15s.; the small parlour got one too, costing £1.[119] He invested in a large mahogany dining table for £3 in July 1745.[120] He had previously purchased a mahogany chest lined with cedar for £4.[121] In December 1745, his purchases included some Windsor chairs, an oak 'scuitore', a mahogany sideboard table and a small round table. Charles was not reluctant to buy good quality second-hand goods, some of his household furniture was bought locally at a cant in Drewstown House, Kells, in April 1743, where he spent £13 3s. 2½d.[122] Charles was especially attached to a particular chair. In March 1746, he paid Banks for 'new lining and mending my chair' and in October he bought a new cushion and had it repaired again.[123] One of his last entries in July 1751 recorded the purchase of a 'blue camblet bed and one pair of window curtains', costing £19 18s. 6d.[124]

Whereas furniture and furnishings, however sumptuous and extravagant, were the necessities of everyday living, pictures and paintings were luxuries. Paintings and prints lightened the feel of the fashionable rooms in the house and were

7 Silver stag brooch. Inscription on presentation box '*Master of the buckhounds to the king of Sardinia*'.

regarded as necessary in gentlemen's houses. In 1745, Charles Tisdall had his portrait painted by Stephen Slaughter (1697–1765), one of the foremost portrait painters of his day, at a cost of £22 15s. He also bought a gilt frame for the painting at £3 0s. 3d.[125] The portrait hung in Mount Tisdall and later in Charlesfort House (fig. 6).[126] In it, Charles is wearing his 'bob wig' purchased in Paris in October 1741 for £1 12s. 6d.[127] He is also sporting a small silver stag brooch, the insignia of his position as *Master of the buckhounds to the king of Sardinia* (fig. 7).[128]

In December 1742, Charles bought two engraved glazed prints from John Brooks, Dublin, engraver, at a cost of £1 8s. 2d.[129] One was of Hugh Boulter DD (1672–1742), the archbishop of Armagh. The archbishop had died the previous September so perhaps Charles bought it for sentimental reasons. The other print was of Henry Boyle (1686–1764), speaker of the house of commons, who, like Charles, also had his portrait painted by Stephen Slaughter.[130] These prints were probably treasured because of Charles' associations with their subjects.[131] In February 1748/9, he purchased three landscapes for £3 8s. 3d. The artist was Mr Lombard.[132] At his uncle James Palmer's auction, Charles bought some pictures drawn by his late uncle.[133]

Such evidence provides testimony to the visibly fashionable side of the 18th century gentleman. Tisdall's expenditure recorded in his account book reveals his outward 'public' façade and how he presented himself to his peers and acquaintances. In 1754, Charles married Hester Cramer.[134] Her inscription on his memorial plaque in Martry Church, the ancestral burial place, gives a summation of her perception of both his public and private life:

> He was a most affectionate, indulgent and tender parent and sincere friend and ardent lover of his country without fear of popularity; charitable without ostentation, an indulgent landlord and benevolent to all mankind. He was beloved and esteemed by all good men and is now and sincerely lamented. He departed this life on the 29 June, 1757, age 37.[135]

Whether he was 'an indulgent landlord' will become clearer in the next chapter.

2. The world of the Tisdall estate

A ccording to Edith Mary Johnson, 'ownership of land was the basis of private wealth, social position and political power' in Ireland during the 18th century.[1] Though Charles derived a substantial income from his many properties in Drogheda and Dublin, it was his ownership of land that bestowed on him his political power and his social position in his own locality, among his tenants, and in Co. Meath at large. In 1672, Michael Tisdall II purchased the manor of Martry, comprising the townlands of Phoenixtown, Jackstowne, Little Athgaine, Nugentstown, Valvinstown, Drissoge and 40 acres in Cortown; with rent out of Staplestown, Jordanstown and Allenstown from Nicholas Darcy at a cost of £1,050 (figs. 8 and 9). A document dated 1741, lists the Tisdall estate as comprising '200 messuages, 200 cottages, 100 gardens, 10 orchards, five castles, five mills and 2,950 acres of land in the townlands of Martry, Hurdlestown, Phoenixtown, Valvinstowne, Great Athgaine, Little Athgaine, Beanstowne, Nugentstown, Possextown, and Mount Tisdall'.[2]

This was not in one large tract of land but geographically straddled the baronies of Upper Kells, Lower Navan and Lune and extended across the civil parishes of Kells, Teltown, Donaghpatrick, Martry, Balrathboyne and Athboy. The Blackwater and its tributary, the Borora, drained it together with the smaller river Ballybeg. The old Navan–Kells coach road separated most of the estate from the demesne house and farm, Mount Tisdall, on its northern boundary. The extent of the estate did not remain constant even during Charles' short tenure; it increased and decreased. In 1745, Charles was busily engaged in purchasing part of the townland of Possextown in the civil parish of Rathcore in the barony of Lower Moyfenrath, in south Co. Meath, some 22 miles distant from his main estate, at a cost of £2,000 (fig. 10). His father had contracted to buy this estate from James Barry.[3] By 1748, Charles had sold Possextown. He may have been motivated by the need to remain solvent and may have needed the money to pay his debts and expenses.[4] He was heavily engaged in building the new demesne house, Charlesfort House, at this time.[5] It also lay a distance from the rest of his estate.

During Charles' minority, the estate had been managed by Charles Hamilton and William Waller, with Robert Waller acting as agent. Charles' father, Michael III, had died in 1727, after a lengthy illness. Robert Waller wrote that Michael had 'left his affairs by his long indisposition in the utmost confusion and disorder', with a 'good part of his lands unsett or in beggars' hands'. Robert's frustration emerged again when he expressed the opinion that his 5 per cent agent's fee should

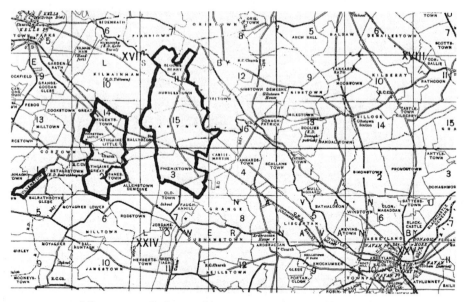

8 Tisdall estate, townlands around Martry. Original manor of Martry on right,
Banestown (outlined south-east of middle plot).

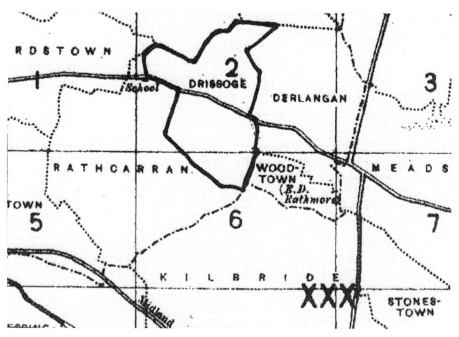

9 Tisdall estate, townland of Drissoge. Michael Tisdall II purchased Drissoge (441a. 1r.
24p.) in 1672. It was leased to Robert Waller from 1 Nov. 1718 to 1739; Drissoge is not
mentioned anywhere in CTAB.

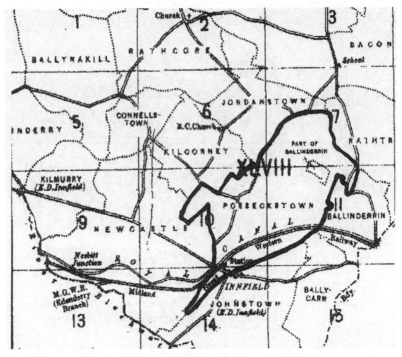

10 Tisdall estate, townland of Possextown.

'not be thought much' considering the time and expense he spent in 'distraining, receiving and other ways seeking for the same' and on his journeys to Dublin 'in paying and accounting Lord Kildare, Mr Henery and the tenants, which accounts were left in the utmost confusion'.[6]

Despite Robert Waller's efforts to restore some order to the affairs of the estate, it may be expected that it was in less than perfect working order when Charles took over its stewardship in 1740. Regarding the lands still held in his own hands, Charles lamented that between May 1740 and May 1746 'the profits were very inconsiderable except to answer the consumption of the house and stables'.[7] This mirrored the economic situation throughout the country and was not peculiar to the Tisdall estate alone. Unlike his father, Charles was very active in the running of his estate and, when not abroad or in Dublin, appears to have supervised it closely, usually acting as his own agent. He was assisted in many aspects of the work by employees under his direction. One of these was Hugh Keowan, from the north of Ireland, sometimes agent, but mostly farm steward, from 1740 to 1751. In 1744, the demesne farm comprised 830 acres held in Charles' own hands.[8]

There is only one record of Hugh's wages during the 11-year-period. He was paid £5 10s. 'in full for wages' in June 1741.[9] Perhaps this was money owing to him from the previous October when Charles came into his inheritance. Hugh dealt with a variety of tasks, buying and selling cattle at fairs, markets and cants. The farm had been devoid of stock from the time of Michael III's death. In an abstract of farm expenses for the year 1744, Charles recorded that 453 sheep, 34 cows and bullocks, eight coach horses and some saddle horses were bought for the 830-acre farm. It is likely that Hugh made these purchases, since Charles spent a lot of time abroad during 1744. Hugh sold two cows for Charles to a butcher in the nearby town of Navan for £5 18s. in January 1740/1 and bought cattle and sheep at the fairs in Kells.[10] He also regularly sold sheep skins, lamb skins and wool from the demesne produce. He was assisted by Simon Willoughby, who may also have been from the north of Ireland and was possibly related to Hugh Willoughby with whom Charles socialized in Swanlinbar.[11] Hugh Keowan and Simon appear to have been trusted and loyal employees and were both rewarded with a 'Christmas box' of £1 2s. 9d. from Charles in December 1741. In May 1743, Charles bought Hugh a silver watch as a present.[12]

Hugh may also, on occasion, have collected the rents. Omission of any recorded rental payments in November 1741 until 27 November may be the only evidence to support this contention. Charles was still in Europe, only returning at the end of the month. It is likely that Hugh collected the rents in his absence, presenting them to Charles, who, on his return, then entered all payments on one day, 27 November. If Hugh received a percentage of the rent monies he collected, as Robert Waller did during Charles Tisdall's minority, no record survives.[13] The estate that Charles inherited was heavily encumbered and burdened with outstanding family settlements, debts and bonds unpaid by and to his father, Michael III (1693–1726) and his grandfather William (1668–1725), settlements that Charles had to honour. Michael III's will decreed that on his death, all stock, moveables, leases and contracts on the estate be sold, the money raised to be invested and the interest accruing to fund a number of bequests and settlements – Charles' mother's jointure, his sister's annual allowance, 'dieting, lodging and washing' for Michael's father, William Tisdall, even paying for 'snuff for the old man'. Unpaid wages and outstanding debts had to be paid; £360 was due to Robert, earl of Kildare, £369 due to his uncle, George Tisdall, all of which greatly reduced Charles' inheritance.[14]

When necessary, Charles employed a number of professional people to assist him in legal matters on 11 recorded occasions during the period 1740 to 1751 (table 2.1). Charles engaged both local and Dublin-based solicitors. On 12 July 1744, Sam Owens, attorney, was paid £12 15s. on account. This was for discharging a bond of £300 sterling given by Charles' father, Michael III, to Revd Mr George Tisdall and George's sister, Catherine Tisdall, on 27 July 1716, payable on the death of his grandfather William Tisdall. The following April, Charles had to resort to the services of James Cane to recover money due by his grandfather William Palmer's bond to his father, Michael.[15] Charles' father, Michael, was married to Catherine Palmer, so perhaps this was part of a marriage

Table 2.1. Lawyers engaged by Charles Tisdall

Lawyer's name	Reason	Date
George Taaffe	Suit commenced by Charles' uncle against him when Charles was a minor	Jan. 1743/4
Sam Owens	Discharging Charles' father's bond	July 1744
James Cane	Recovering money due to Charles' father	Apr. 1745
Attorney Caulfield & Counsellor Parnell	Suit against William Waller	July 1745
Serjeant Tisdall	Drawing up Charles' will	Nov. 1745
Serjeant Tisdall	Examining Charles' titles to Possextown	Feb. 1745/6
Mr McCausland	Drawing deed of mortgage	Feb. 1745/6
Mr Connelly	Dealing with Mr Fortick	Feb. 1745/6
Sam Owens	Purchasing Possextown	Mar. 1745/6
Sub sheriff	Executing writ of *habere* for Possextown	June 1746
Mr Kathrens	Drawing up and putting codicil to Charles' will	Feb. 1748/9

Source: CTAB

settlement. On 30 January 1743/4, Charles engaged the services of his cousin, Serjeant Philip Tisdall (1703–77). A serjeant was a law officer who spoke for his client at litigation hearings.[16] Philip was a noted lawyer and politician, later attorney general in 1760.[17] In January 1744/5, Charles paid him a fee of £10. Charles also had him draw up his will on 24 November 1745, for which the fee was £10.

Another professional, whose services Charles used regularly, was the surveyor, John Bell. He had been employed as a land surveyor and mapper for the Navan–Nobber turnpike road in 1734 and was experienced and reputable.[18] One of Charles' first major administrative initiatives in 1742 was to engage him to survey and lay out his estate at the rate of a penny an acre. Discrepancies and under-calculation of acreage could mean a substantial loss of potential income, so an accurate survey was essential for the new landlord prior to entering into leases and setting rents. The survey, undertaken between July 1742 and July 1743, cost £11 13s. 9d., indicating a 2,805-acre estate surveyed. Later in 1744, Charles paid £5 13s. 9d. 'to Bell for surveying each field of Martry'.[19] Landlords also engaged surveyors to survey disputed land. On 25 March 1745, Charles paid John Bell, £2 5s. 6d. to survey the townland of Banestown. Surrounded on two sides by the Waller estate of Allenstown, the 93-acre townland of Banestown on the Tisdall estate (fig. 8) proved to be a bone of contention between Charles and William Waller, the lessee. William had been executor of the Tisdall estate during Charles' minority (1727–40). His kinsman, Robert, the agent, had held a 21-year lease on Banestown from 1718 until 1739 at 6s. an acre. Perhaps the Waller and Tisdall estate boundaries had become blurred over the years.²⁰ In February 1741/2, Charles wrote to William Waller stating that he was unclear as to where the boundary lay between Allenstown and Banestown and that he would like to have a 'lasting mearing'.²¹ Nothing was done about the mearing until 1743, when Charles discovered its location from one of his tenants, Philip Marky.

An apparently unrelated incident had occurred in 1739 which was to prove significant. The incident was recorded in Charles' account book four years later, when, on 26 December 1743, he paid Philip Marky 13s. 4½d. Charles did not state what the payment was for but recorded the incident related to him by Philip Marky. In 1739, Marky's dog killed a deer of Waller's for which action Waller arrested Marky in Navan market four years later in 1743 and made him pay half a guinea (10s. 6d.) for the deer and 2s. for the action. 'Marky told me he was sure Mr Waller did it in spite to him for having shewn me the mearings of Beanestown'.²² The lapse of four years between the deer-killing incident in 1739 and the arrest in Navan 1743 seems unduly long and would lead one to deduce that perhaps Marky's suspicions were correct. His disclosure of the boundary location may have triggered off the exacting of revenge for the deer-killing incident. The 13s. 4½d. paid by Charles to Marky could perhaps be the re-imbursement of the 12s. 6d. total loss incurred by Marky with the extra 10½d. a token of Charles' gratitude for the information. More likely it represented 2 per cent interest on 12s. 6d. each year for the previous four years. Equipped with this information, Charles set about securing and improving the townland of Banestown. In May 1744, he began building a 10-acre paddock with a mearing ditch and bank. The paddock was surrounded by a seven-foot wall, part of which still survives, and had three sets of piers and gates. It cost £64 15s. John Bell's survey of March 1745 may have served the dual purpose of surveying the disputed boundary and measuring and valuing the land with a view to selling it. Charles later sold the newly built paddock and 43 acres of Banestown to William Waller for £759 18s. 4d.²³

Beyond Mount Tisdall demesne, there were 600 acres in the townlands of Martry, Hurdlestown and Possextown unlet in 1744. This reflected the neglect that Robert Waller, agent, had identified due to a combination of factors; Michael III's prolonged illness when there was 'a good part of his lands unsett or in beggars' hands', his absenteeism on MP duties, and the economic difficulties of the early 1740s, when securing suitable solvent tenants was an up-hill struggle.²⁴ Charles' intention was to lease all the land, except the demesne farm, to generate income. Charles was as dependent on the land as his tenants were. He needed the income from rents to support him; his tenants needed the land to earn their living and maintain their families.²⁵ The lease, at the heart of this landlord tenant relationship, was a contract between landlord and tenant for a grant of property for a certain length of time in return for payment of rent. Conditions and clauses could be inserted in the lease. From Charles' point of view, the lease streamlined

Table 2.2. Tisdall leases, 1740–53

Source	Year	Tenant	Duration	Acres	Townland
CTAB	1743/4	Hugh Lowther	5 years	59	Gerrard's Park
CTAB	1744	Hugh Lowther	28 years	150	Hurdlestown
CTAB	1745	James Flood	31 years	Not stated	Athgaine Little
NLI	1747	Richard Lingham	30 years/ 3 lives	15	Part of Martry Hurdlestown
CTAB	1748	John McKartney	31 years/ 3 lives	25	Part of Martry
CTAB	1748	Charles Pleasants	31 years/ 7 lives	214	Part of Martry
CTAB	*1748	Hugh Lowther	26 years/ ? lives	Not stated	Gerrard's Park, Part of Martry
CTAB	1749	David Scofield	31 years	12	Athgaine Great
CTAB	1749	Peter Kavanagh	31 years	19	1 field in Hurdlestown
CTAB	1749	Richard Lingham	31 years/ 4 lives	Not stated	Island of Hurdlestown
CTAB	1749	Thomas Smyth	31 years	58	Nugentstown
CTAB	1749	Matthew Clerkan	31 years	82	Nugentstown
NLI & RD	1750	Hugh Lowther	5 lives	448	Part Martry Phoenixtown Hurdlestown

Source: CTAB; NLI, microfilm, p. 4692; RD, 143/ 373/ 97381.
*The 1748 lease may have been an extension of the lease agreed in 1743/4.

the management of his estate and cut down on his workload, since he was acting as his own estate agent as well as landlord. Charles executed 13 leases between 1743/4 and 1750 (table 2.2).

From the fragmentary extant records of the Tisdall estate, it is not possible to give a complete picture of land tenure on the estate in the 1740s and 1750s. Some family records that had survived until the 1960s were lost when the estate was sold in 1968 and the family moved to England. Two leases relevant to this study are preserved in the Tisdall papers in the National Library of Ireland, one of the two is also recorded in the Registry of Deeds; 11 further leases have been extrapolated from Charles' account book.[26] The leases in the National Library of Ireland were written on a standard printed form containing 11 headings and stating the tenant's name, the townland in which the holding was located, the date of commencement of the lease, its terms, the names of lives, and the fine upon renewal, if any. In land contracts, a fine was a payment upfront to secure admission to a tenancy, and when leases expired, they were renewed sometimes on payment of a fine. Landlords, experiencing cash-flow problems, as Charles Tisdall and other landlords did in the 1740s, often inserted a fine in the lease clause. They were prepared to forego long-term higher rental income for immediate cash gain. This resulted in land being leased at a lower rent. When Charles leased Martry Mill to Matthew Leigh on 28 February 1744, he reduced the yearly rent from £21 sterling to £19 sterling, provided Matthew pay a fine of £10. He also inserted a fine in his lease to Hugh Lowther on 31 March 1744 for 'eight acres of oats sown and the lease of the small tythe and glebe of Martry during Mr Galliardy's incumbency at seven pounds per annum'.[27] In 1745, James Flood paid the substantial fine of £102 9s. to secure a 31-year lease at the low rent of 10s. per acre (table 2.4).[28]

The first lease, recorded in his account book and agreed during Charles Tisdall's tenure in January 1743/4, was one for five years with Hugh Lowther for a 59-acre field in Phoenixtown, called Gerrard's Park. The second lease, again with Hugh Lowther, was agreed two months later on 31 March 1744. It was for 150 acres in Hurdlestown at 11s. 6d. an acre for 28 years or the lives of Hugh, his wife, Abigail Woodward, their three children or any children he might thereafter have. By April 1744, Charles was anxious to lease two farms, a total of 600 acres of his estate.[29] Perhaps the 600 acres comprised a number of smaller holdings that had been given up due to the 'economic depression'. This happened on Robert French's estate in Monivea in east Co. Galway during the same period.[30] It was a time of economic depression and political uncertainty. An unprecedented frost in winter of 1739–40, followed by severe famine in 1740–1, decimated the population in Ireland.[31] Although advertising land was not considered a desirable option, nevertheless on 24 April 1744 Charles resorted to placing an advertisement in the *Dublin Penny Journal* for 200 acres in Hurdlestown with 'an excellent farm house'. He also advertised 400 acres of land at Martry, describing the holding as 'well inclosed, sheltered and divided with a large old house and a good orchard'. Neither advertisement produced results, however, until 1748 and 1750 respectively. By November 1747, Charles had also advertised the townland of Possextown 14 times.[32] A third lease appears to have been agreed with James Flood on 8 May 1745, when Charles recorded receiving £39 9s. in part payment of the larger fine of £102 9s. for land in Athgaine Little.

A fourth lease was secured on 26 January 1747. Richard Lingham leased 15 acres of Hurdlestown, for 30 years or three lives at half-yearly rent of £5 16s. 3d. However, the lease for three lives was not to commence until 1 May 1749, more than 15 months later. Only one life was recorded, however, that of Ann Fowtherall. The rent was extremely high at 15s. 6d. per acre, so it is not surprising to discover that no fine was paid. The economy was recovering by 1748 and Charles agreed three leases that year. The previously advertised holding at Martry was leased in three lots, one parcel each to Hugh Lowther, Catherine Pleasants and John McKartney, all Protestants. Five more leases were agreed in 1749. It was not until 1750 that the advertised holding at Martry was leased. On 19 January 1750, Hugh Lowther leased part of Martry, part of Hurdlestown and the townland of Phoenixtown, a total of 447 acres 2 roods and 30 perches, for five lives renewable for ever, making him the largest tenant on the estate. The five lives on the lease were: George Lowther, Mary Rothwell, Honourable Hercules Taylor, William Battersby and John Rothwell, all prominent in the area, of whose deaths Charles would be well aware, an important consideration when determining when a life in a lease had ceased. The half-yearly rent was £123 10s. – thus the average rent per acre on this holding was 11s. 4d. This was 2d. per acre lower than Hugh had paid six years earlier in 1744. This may have been in consideration of the inclusion of a £20 fine upon renewal of the lease together with the large acreage of land rented.[33] These 13 leases (table 2.2) represented 40 per cent of the tenants on the estate. All other leases were *in situ* when Charles inherited, so he was obliged to honour them. The leases, together with rental payments recorded in Charles' account book, form the basis for a unique insight into a Co. Meath rural community in the mid-18th century. They capture a snapshot in time on this estate, albeit a snapshot of 11 years' duration.

Under the Act to prevent the further growth of Popery (1704), Catholics were prohibited from holding leases for longer than 31 years. Eight leases on the Tisdall estate during the period under study were for 31 years' duration (table 2.2). Four of these eight leases were to Protestant tenants, Hugh Lowther, Richard Lingham, John McKartney and Charles Pleasants. A fifth lease was to Peter Kavanagh, a blacksmith on the Tisdall estate, who held one 19-acre field in Hurdlestown. He was a Catholic.[34] The religious denomination of the other tenants holding 31-year leases is not known. Another lease was for 30 years or three lives, one was for 28 years, one for 26 years or lives, the number of lives not specified, and there was one lease for five lives. Again this was to Hugh Lowther, who held a total of four of the 13 leases.

On the Tisdall estate in the 1740s and 1750s, there were 33 tenants paying rent directly to Charles Tisdall (table 2.3). Who were the tenants? To understand better the composition of the society that inhabited this estate and the dynamics of the tenantry, it may be useful to subdivide the tenants into five hierarchical groups. At the top of the pyramid were five large farmers, Hugh Lowther, Catherine Pleasants, the widow Flood, Mrs Fleming and William Waller. Hugh Lowther was the son of George Lowther, a former tenant, who held a 21-year lease of land on the Tisdall estate from 1721 and who had taken care of Charles' grandfather, William Tisdall, from 1725 until his death.[35] He was a neighbour of Tisdall's and lived in Hurdlestown House. Catherine Pleasants was a kinswoman of the Tisdall family. She lived in Martry House. William Waller from nearby Allenstown, though a landowner in his own right, was also a tenant of Charles Tisdall. Both the widow Fleming and Mrs Fleming held land continuously during Charles' minority.[36] Most of the estate was let to these tenants. The largest tenant, leasing for the longest time span, was Hugh Lowther. In 1750, he agreed a lease for more than 447 acres. Another large tenant in this group was Mrs Catherine Pleasants, who rented part of Martry and lived in Martry House. The widow Flood appears to have been a substantial tenant too. Her year's rent amounted to £107 0s. 9½d. in November 1740.[37] Estimating her rent at 10s. 6d. per acre, then her holding comprised almost 204 acres.[38]

Landlords could also be tenants on other estates – Charles rented the townland of Possextown from 1740 until he purchased it on 11 March 1745/6.[39] William Waller rented from Charles the townland of Banestown with seven houses and gardens and three acres of potato ground. The seven houses may have been sub-let to smaller tenants. They were possibly cabins since there were no houses in Banestown by 1836.[40] The townland, containing 93 acres, adjoined both estates and down the years was a bone of contention and the subject of a law case between the two landowners. In 1745 Charles paid a fee of £5 13s. 9d. to the attorney general for hearing a suit against Waller.[41] Two of the above-named large tenant farmers, Hugh Lowther and Mrs Fleming, were also middlemen, renting to sub-tenants (table 2.3). Hugh Lowther appears to have sub-let part of his farm in Phoenixtown to William and John Donaghoo and a further part to Patrick King and William Marky. In November 1741, King and Marky paid £21 4s., for a half year's rent. Hugh was renting his land from Charles Tisdall at 10s. 6d. an acre. It is likely that his subtenants paid more. Patrick McCabe was another sub-tenant of Hugh Lowther. Lawrence Balfe was a sub-tenant of Mrs Fleming.

The second group on the hierarchical scale were the tenants who held land in partnerships, where each member was responsible for paying his own share of the rent, the partnership being accountable for defaulters. There is evidence of three partnerships on the estate. In 1741, James Mooney, Bryan Hartford, Patrick Dooley and Patrick Donaghree together rented Athgaine Great. They each paid £11 8s. 3d. rent on the same day, 17 March. In November 1741, Bryan Hartford, Patrick Dooley and Patrick Donaghree were still leasing Athgaine Great, paying £35 8s. for a half-year's rent. Patrick Mooney seems to have left the partnership. Calculating rent at 10s. 6d. per acre in 1741, this holding was in excess of 141 acres. In March 1741/2, William Marky and Patrick King also held land in partnership in Phoenixtown. William paid his share on 26 March 1741/2, while Patrick paid his account four days later on 30 March. In January 1748, another partnership emerged, that of Matthew Clerkan and the Caffreys who paid Charles £23 8s. for a half year's rent.[42]

Lower down the hierarchy still was the third group, the tenants with smaller holdings, who worked on the estate and demesne farm, a mutually beneficial arrangement. They paid part of their rent in labour, thus guaranteeing the landlord a readily accessible work-force. It also ensured that rent could be paid in kind and goes some way towards explaining the low cash turnover in Charles' account book. John Nowland, the mason, a case in point, leased seven acres in Hurdlestown and often paid his rent in labour. On one occasion, he paid his rent before the due date, because he had received cash for his mason's work.[43] John

McKartney regularly paid his rent in cash, labour and butter.[44] Further down the scale again were cotters such as Thady Nall, John Reilly and Thady Mucklevaney. Thady Mucklevaney exchanged his labour for two-and-a-half acres of potato ground to pay the high rent of 12s. an acre in 1741 (table 2.4). In the fifth group at the very bottom of the pyramid were many others, such as Patrick Gallahor, the weaver, who paid £1 for a year's grazing for a cow in 1742, and William Maglew, who also paid £1 for grazing in April 1744.[45] Letting land for grazing boosted Charles' income by £59 5s. during the year May 1744 to May 1745.[46]

In theory, Charles Tisdall should have been able to accurately forecast his rental income due on the two gale days, 1 May and 1 November, and balance his books accordingly. In reality, rental payments were irregular and sporadic especially in the difficult early years of the 1740s. Arrears of rent ranged from two to 18 months, the most usual time lapse between due date and payment date being six or seven months. Hugh Lowther made four piecemeal payments between 2 September and 15 October 1740. He paid in a similar manner in November the following year.[47] From 1742 onwards, though, Hugh Lowther always paid his rent seven months after the due date, paying the November rent the following June and the May rent in December.[48] It was difficult for smaller tenant farmers and cotters to realize cash for rent when they needed it. They were dependent on too many external factors such as weather and the fluctuations of supply and demand at markets. In January 1743/4, Thady Nall, a cotter, paid Charles outstanding rent, due 14 months earlier in November 1742.

It is difficult to ascertain any significant pattern of rents or rental increases on the estate during the period 1740 to 1751, due to the absence of a rent book for the period. Charles' account book is a record of receipts and payments only, and rental payments are included among a myriad of other receipts, such as payment for work on the turnpike road, interest received on loans and money won playing cards. Even though there was continuity of tenantry on the Tisdall estate, very few rentals can be traced for the entirety of the period under study. In many cases the acreage of the holdings remains unknown and only the monetary payments are recorded. It is, however, possible to establish the rents per acre in the 1730s, since Robert Waller, the agent during Charles' minority, kept accounts. Robert paid 6s. per acre rent to the Tisdall estate for the townlands of Banestown (fig. 8) and Drissoge (fig. 9) until 1739, when a 21-year lease on the property expired. 7s. per acre was the rent that the tenants-at-will, Laurence Flood and Thomas Fleming, paid for their holdings in 1730s. This rent was to be increased to 9s. an acre in 1740 when 'the minor (Charles) comes of age'.[49] Charles valued the lands held in his own hands at 10s. an acre between 1740 and 1746.[50] Patrick Donaghree, Patrick Dooly & Bryan Hartford paid 'half a guinea per acre', 10s. 6d. on 23 Mar. 1740/1.[51]

The only certainty that can be established is that rents increased during the period (table 2.4). Population growth after 1740 increased demand for land and drove up rental prices. However, there were troughs and peaks within this decade too; on the whole, rents were lower between 1740 and 1746 and rose between

Table 2.3. Tenants on Tisdall estate, 1740–51

	Tenant	Townland
1	Hugh Lowther	Gerrard's Park, Hurdlestown, Martry
2	James Holgan 1744-5	Martry Mill
3	Patrick Doyle 1745-6	Martry Mill
4	Matthew Leigh 1746-51	Martry Mill
5	Matthew Clerkan	Calf Park
6, 7, 8, 9	Bryan Hartford, Patrick Dooly, Patrick Donaghree, James Mooney	Athgaine Great
10	Thomas Casserly	Athgaine Great
11, 12	William & John Donaghoo sub-tenants	Phoenixtown
13	Mrs Fleming	Volvenstown
14	Lawrence Balfe sub-tenant	Volvenstown
15	John Reilly	Not stated
16	Thady Nall	Athgaine Great
17	John McKartney	Part Martry
18	Widow Flood	Part Nugentstown, Athgaine Little
19	William Waller	Banestown
20	Philip Marky	Martry
21	Mrs Pleasants	Martry
22	James Mooney	Athgaine Great
23, 24	John & Philip Skelly	Martry
25	John Nowlan	Hurdlestown
26	Thady Mucklevaney	Athgaine Great
27	Brigid Maglew	Mount Tisdall
28	Caffreys	Part Nugentstown
29	Patrick McCabe	Paddock, part Banestown
30	John Gambell	Part Hurdlestown
31	Patrick King & William Marky	Part Phoenixtown
32	Roger Rhodes	Possexstown
33	Richard Lingham	Island of Hurdlestown

Source: CTAB

1747 and 1751. Since Charles' income was derived mainly from rent, increases, where possible, were essential so that he could develop his estate and support his lifestyle as a landed country gentleman. He needed to ensure that his estate was leased at the highest available rent to the most financially secure tenants who would pay regularly and on time. There were two opportunities for Charles to increase his tenants' rent; annually in the case of the tenants-at-will, and on the execution of a new lease. He undertook 13 such leases during the period under study (table 2.2). Rents were not uniform on the Tisdall estate; the variations

Table 2.4. Rentals, 1739–50

Tenant	Period	Rent	Fine
Robert Waller	1718–39	6s.	not stated
Laurence Flood & Thomas Fleming	1732	7s.	not stated
John Lowther	1736	7s.	not stated
Laurence Flood & Thomas Fleming	1740	9s.	not stated
Patrick Donaghree, Patrick Dooly &			
Bryan Hartford	1740/1	10s. 6d.	not stated
Thady Mucklevaney	1741	12s.	not stated
Thomas Casserly	1741	16s.	not stated
Hugh Lowther	1741	9s. 9d.	not stated
Roger Rhodes	1743	10s.	yes
Lands in Charles Tisdall's own hands	1740–6	10s.	his own land
Hugh Lowther	1744	11s. 6d.	yes
James Flood	1745	10s.	yes
Richard Lingham	1747	15s. 6d.	no
Elizabeth Fleming	1748	14s.	not stated
Thomas Smyth	1749	11s. 11d.	yes
David Scofield	1749	15s.	yes
Matthew Clerkan	1749	11s. 11d.	yes
Hugh Lowther	1750	11s. 4d.	yes

Source: RWAB and CTAB

were almost as numerous as its 33 tenants (table 2.3). Many factors affected this. Preferential terms were agreed with different categories of tenants. Kinship with the landlord, a long lease, a large holding and payment of a fine on renewal of the lease all contributed to a tenant paying lower rent. Kinswoman Catherine Pleasants, and Hugh Lowther, a large gentlemen farmer, were given lower rents. An improving tenant was desirable. Even though 'a solvent client' offered Charles 11s. an acre for his lands in Possextown he preferred letting it to Roger Rhodes at 10s. an acre 'as he had much improved the land by draining during his last lease'.[52] Matthew Leigh of Martry Mill who was prepared to pay a substantial fine to secure a tenancy also enjoyed more favourable rent.[53] Contrariwise, no fine meant very high rent as in the case of Richard Lingham who paid 15s. 6d. an acre in 1747 (table 2.4).

Despite the number of variables in deciding rents and the absence of a rent book, it is still possible, in a few cases, to trace rental fluctuations for particular holdings where the acreage is known and the rents paid recorded. The rentals of four representative holdings, those of Thady Nall, cotter, John Nowland, stone mason, Thomas Casserly, small farmer and the Martry Mill holding can be analysed. These were all tenants-at-will and held no lease. Consequently their rents could be increased or decreased as and when the landlord decided. The largest rent increase of all was suffered by Thady Nall, the cotter, a tenant-at-will. His rent was raised in 1742 and again in 1750. Between 1742 and 1751 the increase was almost 200 per cent. John Nowland was a stone mason on the estate, building much of the stonework that survives to this day: walls, paddocks and a pound, as well as the new demesne house, Charlesfort House. He regularly paid his rent in labour. His rent, the second-highest of the four under analysis, was increased on two occasions and was doubled between 1744 and 1751, perhaps because of improvements that were made to his holding. Thomas Casserly, another tenant-at-will, farmed 24 acres. In 1740, he paid £15 7s. rent or 12s. 9½d. an acre. This was increased by 30 per cent in 1742, and then remained constant until 1749, when it was again raised. Casserly's rent increase in the period 1741–9 was 38 per cent, the second-lowest of four holdings under study, lower than that of the cotter and the tradesman.

The Martry Mill holding changed hands three times in the period 1744–6. Earlier tenants-at-will may have neglected the upkeep of the mill holding, because in 1744 Charles described it as 'out of repair and the land very poor'. Perhaps this was in large measure due to the severity of prevailing climatic and economic conditions and the harvest failure of 1744. Because of this, in 1744 the rent was reduced by 6 per cent. An inscription on the wall of the mill says that it was extended in 1745. Subsequent to the improvements, the rent was increased by 22 per cent that year.[54] This 22 per cent, however, conceals a higher percentage increase because the incoming tenant Matthew Leigh paid a fine of £20 and had the rent reduced by £2 from £21 to £19 as a result. The rent remained constant until 1749. The evidence of these four holdings suggests that a hierarchy existed when determining rent increases. The mill holder was penalized the least, followed by the small farmer and the tradesman; the cotter suffered the greatest increase at 200 per cent. Perhaps though, the higher percentage increases reflected previously very low rents.

In conclusion, it is clear that Charles Tisdall carefully established a successful structured management system on his estate in the period 1740–51, an estate that had been neglected for years. In agreeing 13 leases, he eased the burden of management. He leased two large previously unlet holdings, Martry and Hurdlestown, advertising them to obtain tenants. He purchased, leased and resold Possextown. He secured higher rents on the estate and re-stocked the demesne farm. Yet despite all this, his account book concluded in July 1751 'by balance resteth cash £1 9s.'[55] The young landlord was asset-rich but cash-poor. His total receipts for the month were £152 3s. 6d.; his expenses £150 14s. 6d. But camouflaged beneath these figures were the huge improvements that Charles had undertaken on the estate. He had built a new demesne house, a linen 'factory' for the estate workers and upgraded the infrastructure on the estate, improving roads, bridges and drains. He had planted thousands of trees and constructed boundary ditches. Charles was an 'improving' landlord.

3. An improving landlord

The perception of 'improvement' as 18th-century landowners understood it, was the progressive 'restructuring [of] the landscape for social and economic, as well as aesthetic ends and, by extension, restructuring the conduct of those who lived in, worked in and looked upon it'.[1] The concept of 'improvement' coincided with Charles Tisdall's coming of age. It is possible, though unlikely, that at the age of 21, he arrived back in Ireland from the Grand Tour with a well-developed sense of the new improving philosophy, never mind a blueprint in hand for implementing that improvement as understood by the above definition. He hardly knew his estate, having left it aged seven and living in Dublin until he attained his majority. But, nevertheless, whatever his motives and plans, or lack of them, were, he embraced the ideas of improvement with gusto.

National circumstances contributed to his becoming an improving landlord. A number of significant developments that probably pushed him in this direction began in the early part of the century. The Linen Board had been set up in 1711 to promote local linen industry. The Dublin Society had been founded in 1731 to promote and develop agriculture, arts, industry and science in Ireland and an 'improving' ethos prevailed during the period. The Incorporated Society for promoting English Protestant working schools in Ireland had been granted its charter in 1733/4, resulting in the building of charter schools. The 18th century was also the golden age of building, when construction of the 'big house' flourished. There was a distinct change, too, in what was considered fashionable demesne design, with a move away from the old formal layouts towards 'naturalized' parkland, reflecting a new appreciation that the natural features of woods, rivers and hills were intrinsically beautiful. The Grand Tour exposed Charles to broader perspectives and fresh philosophies as did his close associations with powerful and improving landlords and relatives in Ireland.

The improving ethos fitted in well with the Tisdall estate's needs in the 1740s. The estate was ripe for developing and Charles recognized that the national movements promoting improvement could provide the conduit. Like the rest of Ireland, the estate had been ravaged by the disastrous weather conditions of the early 1740s with resultant poor crops, poverty, famine and disease. The estate needed to be more profitable. The generation of supplementary income for landlord and tenant alike was a pressing financial necessity and was the spur to Charles' building initiatives, tree planting, infrastructural improvements and the establishment of a linen 'factory'. In turn they provided employment for his tenants, enabling them to pay their rent, as well as setting a positive example for 'those who lived in, worked in and looked upon' the landscape.[2] The demesne house at Mount Tisdall had not been occupied by the family since the death of his father in 1727, and rarely lived in even by him, so needed refurbishment. Charles also added all the elements of a fashionable 18th-century demesne, including a boathouse, an ornamental walled garden and thousands of trees. Two years after coming into his inheritance, in the fashion of the day, he began work on a new demesne house, Charlesfort House, although tradition holds that health reasons may also have been a contributory factor. The Tisdalls were a staunch Protestant family; many were clergymen including his cousin, the outspoken vicar of Belfast, the Revd William Tisdall. Charles' motivation for supporting a local charter school at Ardbraccan may have stemmed not only from the prevailing improving ethos of the day, but also from a deep personal faith and religious commitment.

'Improvement' was the precept by which Charles Tisdall lived his life on his Meath estate and the improving mentality of the period 1740 to 1751 was the environment in which he carried it out.[3] Popular publications advised landlords to reside on their estates and manage them, thus improving the condition of their tenants and resulting in the overall improvement of the country. For the tenants where the landlord resided permanently on the estate, 'the regular consumption demands from what was invariably the wealthiest local family reverberated throughout the community, giving employment and a doorstep market for food and fuel'.[4] Charles was never an absentee landlord except to travel abroad, and his travelling decreased as his interests in the estate took over. Unlike his father and many of his relatives, he was neither a lawyer nor a member of parliament, although it is possible he would have entered parliament had he lived long enough.[5] Consequently, his time was not divided between parliament, the courts and his estate, so all his energies went into his estate in building initiatives, tree planting, the promotion of the linen industry and, to a lesser extent, what might be termed moral improvement.

Since there was a parallel between income, rank and the splendour of a gentleman's residence, Charles may have felt that he needed a much grander house than Mount Tisdall. It had rarely been the primary residence of the earlier Tisdall landlords. Many Tisdall owners died young and only occupied the house for short periods. Charles' father, Michael III, spent much of his time in Dublin. The Darcy family, who owned the land for 300 years prior to the Tisdalls, had their seat at Plattin, near Drogheda. By the 1740s, peace and tranquillity had reigned in Ireland for the previous half century after the turbulence of the 17th century, and the resulting stability manifested itself in a house-building boom among the landed gentry. The 'big' house served a social purpose. It demonstrated to peers and tenants alike the wealth and position, standing and taste, of its owner and was a centre for entertainment and hospitality. In 1742, Charles Tisdall embarked on the construction of a new demesne house in Athgaine Little, which he named Charlesfort House after himself (fig. 11). He had two further building projects in hand at the same time: on-going refurbishment work on Mount Tisdall and demesne, to make it suitable for gentlemanly living, and the renovation of his Dublin properties ran concurrently with the building of Charlesfort House.[6]

BUILDING INITIATIVES

Many landowners at the time considered themselves to be amateur architects and were well versed in architectural styles. Reading architectural books was popular and provided inspiration. In September 1742, Charles purchased *Vitruvius Britannicus*, together with Ware's four volumes of *Palladio's architecture*, with a view to building a new house on the estate.[7] Throughout this period, a new fashion of visiting 'big' houses had become popular in Ireland. Mrs Delaney and Dean Swift, Tisdall's contemporaries, were among such tourists.[8] Charles probably visited his relatives, the Kildares, in their newly built Carton House in Maynooth, Co. Kildare. In 1739, Robert, 19th earl of Kildare, Charles' granduncle, commissioned Richard Castle (1690–1751), the foremost architect of his day, to rebuild Carton House. Richard Castle also drew plans for Charles' neighbour, Thomas Taylor, for Headfort House in Kells, which were rejected. He also designed plans for the bishop of Meath's residence at Ardbraccan, which lay adjacent to Charlesfort House and in whose church the Tisdall family had a pew.[9]

In 1742, Charles put in train plans to build himself the new house. He started accumulating materials piecemeal for its construction over a nine-year-period. He had gathered quite a substantial hoard before he engaged Richard Castle to design a plan costing £22. 'To Mr Richard Castle when he gave me the plan for my house. I bargained with him for twenty guineas for his plan, & a guinea every day he overlook'd the execution £20'.[10] The initial plan was for three sides of a square and a tower in front of house. Charles built the tower and back piece, but the wings were never built. The tower was pulled down in 1798 'lest the rebels should get into it and fire down the house from the higher floor.'[11]

Charles always referred to the new house as 'the building'. The first mention of it was in April 1742, when he recorded spending £22 13s. 10d. 'for work done towards the building'.[12] The avenue to Charlesfort House was laid out in the summer of 1742 by John Townshend. Charles must have been pleased with the work because he gave John a present of £1 2s. 9d. 'for laying out the avenue road'.[13] In November Charles purchased 1,000 slates from Ballyjamesduff in Co. Cavan and in December he bought 3,000 bog laths.[14] Between April and December 1742, Charles spent £207 6s. 8d. on materials.[15] This excluded money spent on labour.[16] The best way to improve the lot of the peasantry was to provide work for them.[17] The building of Charlesfort House created employment for many on his estate and the real cost of the building is camouflaged in Charles' account book under monies paid to workmen and estate rents paid in lieu, by labour and goods. For nine years, while the new house was being built, the

11 The present Charlesfort House, rebuilt 1813.

demand for labour and building materials must have boosted the community economy.[18] Apart from unskilled estate tenants and workmen used as labourers on the building of the house, large numbers of tradesmen were also employed (table 3.1).

The 1836 Ordnance Survey map of Athgaine Little shows several quarries, including a quarry in the garden at Charlesfort House and the 'black quarry' in Banestown, possibly so called to distinguish it from 'the white quarry' in nearby Ardbraccan, which supplied cut stone for many Irish buildings.[19] Charles retained the rights to the quarries on his estate, as his lease to Hugh Lowther confirms. Hugh had the use of the lands excepting 'all mines, minerals, quarries, royalties and timber trees'.[20] Consequently, Charles was able to obtain building material, free of charge, on his own property or from Ardbraccan, thereby cutting down on transport costs. The proximity of Ardbraccan quarry also meant that skilled workers such as quarrymen, stone masons and stone cutters were available locally and in plentiful supply. Thirty pounds of gunpowder were used for quarrying on one occasion. Charles made several payments to quarrymen. Michael Quin received £8 19s. for drawing stone from the quarry in the garden at the rate of a penny per load. This represented 2,148 loads of stone.[21] Mount Tisdall demesne also boasted a limestone quarry known as the Limekiln Field, which was very useful for all building work.[22] Although Charles expended money on engaging the architect Richard Castle, he saved a considerable amount by making the bricks for the building on his estate. One Yates was Charles Tisdall's brickmaker. Between June 1746 and October 1748 he made in excess of 92,124 bricks and 3,800

Table 3.1. Tradesmen employed on building Charlesfort House, 1742–51

Name	Trade
Richard Castle	architect
Henry Darley	plasterer/stoneworker
John Nowland	mason
Maurice Tyrrel	mason
— Yates	brick maker
Michael Quin	quarryman
John Townshend	avenue/road maker
Bryan Matthews	kitchen slater
— Toole	glazier
James Tandy	ironmonger
— Turner	ironmonger
Read & Sheridan	builders
— Malone	slater
John Bowler	carpenter
William Reilly	painter
John Bowler	carpenter
Henry McCabe	carpenter & builder

Source: CTAB

tiles.[23] Charles provided the fire for firing the bricks, purchasing tons of coal from the port town of Drogheda, 20 miles away, for the process.[24] During the summer of 1747 six-and-a-half tons of coal costing £8 2s. 6d. was bought for burning the bricks.[25]

The kitchen was in the basement of the house and work began on it in September 1746 and continued for 16 months until January 1747/8. Bryan Matthews slated and rendered the kitchen for which he received £2 4s. in September 1746.[26] He later paved the kitchen yard which cost £1 2s. 9d.[27] In October, 72 feet of glass cost £3.[28] Kitchens in 'the big house' needed a bell and Charles bought a large one with chain and brakes for £3 18s. 9½d. in November 1746.[29] The kitchen hearth was of Ardbraccan stone and Charles paid Maurice Tyrrel £2 12s. for it in January 1747/8.[30] In total, the kitchen cost £13 11s. 6½d. Charles engaged only the foremost craftsmen. One of his stonecutters was Henry Darley (1721–98), who also worked on the Dublin Custom House.[31] In November 1743, Charles paid him for stonecutting work.[32] On 23 December 1744 he paid him a further £7 9s. for a marble chimney piece and several hearth stones.[33] A trawl through Charles' account book reveals that payments towards building Charlesfort House amounted to £522 7s. 2½d. between April 1742 and March 1751. Although Charlesfort House was ready for occupation in 1751, Charles was still living in Mount Tisdall in September of that year.[34]

12 Three cottages built by Charles Tisdall. CTAB, 12 June 1749; it is probable that these are three of the cottages built by Charles Tisdall in 1749 and that the '*c*.1746' date inscribed on a wall plaque is incorrect. The original cottages are to the left in the photograph, the doors were where three large windows are now, the addition to the right with door is an extension, built when the cottages were restored in 2006.

Mount Tisdall had to be maintained as a fit and fashionable gentleman's residence in the interim. In 1728, Robert Waller had paid Christopher Malone for 'thatching the house and outhouses at Mount Tisdall'.[35] On 28 February 1740/1, shortly after inheriting the estate, Charles needed a slater to point Mount Tisdall and its stables, at a cost of £1 11s. 6d.[36] In November, he 'paid Malone the slater in full for work £1 2s. 5½d.', probably to repair the roof.[37] The big parlour needed wainscotting, costing £2 5s. 6d. on 28 February 1743/4.[38] In June 1751, when the new demesne house, Charlesfort House, was ready for occupation, Charles paid William Reilly £9 to paint Mount Tisdall, probably prior to his letting the house to John Murray.[39] Charles also built and improved tenants' houses on his estate. In January 1743/4, he purchased materials for cabins on his estate.[40] Five years later he had John Nowland, his mason, build five labourers' cabins at a cost of £1 14s. 1½d. (fig. 12).[41] One Smyth was paid £1 8s. 5d. for thatching them.[42]

In addition to these five houses, Charles ensured the construction of a sixth by inserting a clause in a lease.[43] On 26 January 1747, Charles agreed to return three guineas in the first half year's rent, or before, to Richard Lingham or his heirs, if improvements were made in the form of a house. Two years later, Charles returned the promised money to Richard's heir, Gambell, towards the cost of building his house in Hurdlestown Island, 'which money I got from and was oblig'd to give it back to him or his heirs for improvements'.[44] Charles also had

Martry House painted in May 1745 and repaired in 1750 at a cost of £5, possibly prior to leasing it to his relative, Catherine Pleasants.[45]

The kitchen garden was located close to the house in Mount Tisdall. In February 1743/4, Charles paid £3 15s. 10d. for 130 feet of glass for a hot bed, packing cost a further 17s. 6d.[46] Walled gardens were built as an integral part of house and demesne design. Charles built impressive walled gardens at Mount Tisdall, which still survive. In December 1746, he paid John Nowland £5 4s. 2d. for building 125 perches of garden wall arched and lined with brick.[47] Two years later, John Nowland was paid £7 17s. 4d. for a wall of similar specifications. This wall cost £4 1s. 0d. Gardens often incorporated statuary and other Renaissance elements. Charles was aware of this trend. In May 1747 while in Italy, he bought a statue of Venus, two urns for the boathouse and four plaster busts for which he paid £7 19s. 3d. Carriage to the ship cost two guineas and carriage from London cost a further 13s. on 19 February 1747/8.[48] The freight and duty on these items set him back a further £3 4s. 4d.[49] Maurice Tyrrel made two pedestals for the urns when he was making stone caps for the piers. These cost two guineas.[50] The previous January Charles had paid him £1 for a dial post of Ardbraccan stone.[51]

Landlords sometimes enhanced their demesnes and gardens with follies, such as at Tollymore, Headfort and Heywood.[52] Some were functional; others whimsical, but all reflected a sensibility to the fashion of the period. Charles added a variety of features to his demesne. He paid John Nowland 'for building a footbridge across the little river' (fig. 13) and added a boathouse (fig. 5) to Mount Tisdall.[53] Such features were intended to pander to aesthetic sensibilities. Charles' third house-improvement project was on his Dublin properties and is outside the scope of this study.

In September 1748, Charles engaged John Nowland, his regular mason, to build a pound on the estate, alongside the main Navan–Kells turnpike road and across the road from Martry Mill. In this enclosure, cattle and other animals could be detained, either as a penalty for trespass and causing damage, or as an indemnity against debt or default. The stock was later released on payment of a fine. The manor of Martry had its own courts leet and baron in 1748, and it may be assumed that animals were impounded there for trespass during Charles' tenure, as they were between 1789 and 1792 in his son Michael III's time. In November 1792, an entry in the court book refers to a court case where John Mitchell's cattle were left in the pound of Martry following trespass and damages done to corn, assessed by the court's appraizer at 14s.10d.[54] John Nowland was paid 8d. per perch and a total of £1 16s. 4d. for building the pound.[55]

Charles also built a 10-acre paddock in Banestown, surrounded by a seven-foot high wall as part of the improvement. The circumference of the paddock was 166 perches. 144 barrels of lime were used on the wall coping, possibly from the limekiln at Mount Tisdall. The wall had three sets of piers and gates, the gate hinges and locks alone cost the substantial sum of £33 12s. 6d.[56] The work

13 Footbridge.

commenced in May 1744 and continued until 1748. Hiring workers to quarry and draw the stone to the paddock cost 4*d.* a perch. Charles also drew 44 perches of material to the site with his own carts at 'a groat a perch', a groat being the equivalent of 4*d.* Several masons were engaged on the work and the amount expended in 1744 was £54 5*s.* 3*d.* In 1748 he paid 'to different masons on account of above work £57 8*s.*'[57] Charles improved Martry churchyard, the family burial place, in June 1744. John Nowland built a five-foot wall around it at 6*d.* per perch, costing £3 11*s.* 3*d.* Pillars of Kilkenny stone cost an extra £4 9*s.* 10*d.*[58] The churchyard wall still stands intact. The old demesne house was less fortunate. Much of the fabric of the present Bloomsbury House, alias Mount Tisdall, may be attributable to the 19th century when the house was greatly enlarged and refashioned by the Kells builder, Francis Nulty, for Richard Barnewell.[59]

TREE PLANTATION

Trees were unquestionably the distinguishing hallmark of the demesne landscape and tree planting was a component element of 18th-century improvement. In many places hedges and trees that had survived until the 1740s were used for fuel during the harsh climatic conditions of 1740 and 1741.[60] In the poem, *Cill Cais*, the writer lamented the disappearance of the forests

> Cad a dhéanfaimid feasta gan adhmad?
> Tá deireadh na gcoillte ar lár[61]

('now what will we do for timber, with the last of the woods laid low?').

The great forests had almost disappeared; there were 50 acres of woods, less than 2 per cent, on the Tisdall estate in 1741. What Charles referred to as 'the ash tree park of Athgaine' may have constituted some of those 50 acres.[62] Tree planting was given a boost in the 1740s when the Dublin Society offered premiums for the greatest number of trees planted.[63] The Society encouraged landowners and tenants to plant newly introduced hardwoods, such as sycamore, beech, walnut, lime and horse chestnut. Tree plantation served a number of purposes. Trees and hedges defined the perimeters of estates and townlands. They enhanced the landscape; gentlemen's houses were identified by their tree-lined avenues and plantations, 'for the house of the planter is known by the trees'.[64] They provided shelterbelts for property and livestock, and were used for fuel and building materials. By 1750, Charles Tisdall had planted 11,240 trees comprising 3,040 ash and elm trees, 2,000 birch, 1,200 beech, 3,000 Dutch alder and in excess of 2,000 oak trees. He also planted a number of other 'forest' trees at a cost of £10 10s. 11d. Tree planting created welcome employment for gardeners and labourers alike. Trees needed tending after planting. On 27 August 1748, Charles paid 'Keightly a gardiner for spending three days in nailing up my wall fruit trees £1 2s. 9d.[65] On another occasion, on 28 February 1748/9, he paid Magonan & Smyth 'for dressing my fruit trees £1 11s. 6d.' John Paine planted 16 ash trees 'in the labourers' gardens in Moat roe' for 11s. 4½d.[66] The Dublin Society also promoted the construction of ditches set with hawthorn hedges, with trees planted at regular intervals. On 11 April 1749, John Paine received 17s. 6d. for planting 'the labourers' garden ditch in Moatroe' on the estate.[67] Charles purchased 157,000 whitethorn quicks and 5,000 crab apple quicks together with a barrel of holly berries presumably to plant in hedges.[68] Quicks were between 18 inches and 2 feet in height so it would take some years before they made an impact on the landscape. Orchards were also a feature of demesnes. In January 1740/1 Charles paid Michael Kinsella £3 19s. 2d. for 150 apple trees and 50 pear trees.[69] Two years later he planted peach and apricot trees and some wall trees.

INFRASTRUCTURE

Improving roads and bridges was regarded as important 'improvement' work as it led to a better and speedier communication network. It facilitated cheaper transport costs for goods and personnel alike, lessened the wear and tear on carts and wagons and benefitted the local economy. Charles' contribution to road improvement may be divided into two categories. The first entailed work sought and contracted for from the Meath grand jury; the second was work undertaken on the Navan–Kells turnpike road, both of which effected improvement on the Tisdall estate. The grand juries in each county controlled local government and levied rates for the upkeep of the roads and the building and maintenance of public buildings. Officially they were appointed by the county sheriff and comprised the county's prominent residents and landlords. Charles Tisdall was a member of the Meath grand jury in March 1745/6, attending the first day of the assizes in Trim on Monday 1 March 1745/6, where John Pratt also attended. It is likely that he continued to be a member until his untimely death.[70] Charles was included in a list of subscribers towards producing a grand jury map and survey of the county, and along with Thomas Taylor, pledged £5 13s. 9d. towards its compilation.[71] In his account book, Charles recorded his expenses at the assizes. His yearly bill for lodgings with Mrs Evans in Trim cost £1 10s. in 1743 and a similar amount again in 1749; his bill from her husband for soap and candles was a more substantial £2 16s.[72] However, his attendances at the assizes were profitable and he secured lucrative road contracts in the years between 1744 and 1750. In addition, he was appointed overseer on a number of the roads, which brought in an extra 5 per cent income.

First, Charles identified roads and bridges around his estate that were in need of repair. Between October 1744 and July 1746, Charles submitted and was awarded four presentments from the Meath grand jury. The roads may have been in poor condition by that time, having been eroded badly perhaps during the early 1740s due to harsh weather conditions. Two of these presentments were for work on Banestown Bridge. Why Banestown Bridge at this juncture in time? It lay beside the new demesne house, Charlesfort House, which Charles was in the throes of building at the time. It was on the road to the Waller home in Allenstown House, where he socialized, Ardbraccan Church, where he worshipped, and Trim, where he attended the assizes. The raw materials of stone, gravel, sand and lime were readily and economically available in Banestown quarry and in the many other quarries on the estate. Prior to an application to the grand jury for funding to repair roads and bridges, the proposed work had to be planned and costed. Charles recorded one occasion when he proposed laying out a new road to Ardbraccan. He always engaged personnel of the highest calibre and in June 1751, he paid John Bell, his surveyor, previously a surveyor and mapper for the Navan–Nobber turnpike road, £1 2s. 9d. 'for laying out an intended road to Ardbraccan'.[73] The outcome of this project remains unknown, since Charles' account book ceased the following month in July 1751. In total, Charles received £127 4s. 0d. (table 3.2) over a six-year-period from the grand jury. The grand jury was also responsible for the upkeep of bridges. Charles gave Gustavus Lambart Esq. a subscription of £11 7s. 6d. in April 1743 towards a 'bridge across the Boyne at Bray ford'.[74] Five years later, in November 1748, he gave £5 13s. 9d. towards Tankardstown Bridge across the Blackwater.[75]

An act in 1710 had extended the authority of grand juries to spend money on the repair and construction of roads.[76] However, the increased volume of traffic of the early 18th century found the county grand juries unable to finance the spate of road-building needed. Acts of Parliament had established a tolled turn-pike road from Dublin to Navan in 1729 and its continuation from Navan to Kells in 1733. These acts enabled the trustees to raise funds by way of debentures from

Table 3.2. Road and bridge work

Date	Grand jury	Turnpike trust	Work
4 Oct. 1744	£25 0s. 0d.		Banestown bridge
22 May 1745		£2 0s. 0d.	battlements on turnpike bridge
5 Mar. 1745/6	£7 18s. 8d.		road at Banestown
5 Mar. 1745/6	£3 0s. 0d.		bridge at Martry
15 July 1746	£23 6s. 8d.		repairing road to turnpike
4 Mar. 1749	£15 0s. 0d.		footbridge across the Blackwater ford
15 June 1749		£2 7s. 0½d.	work on turnpike
7 July 1749		£13 0s. 1½d.	turnpike road
19 Sept. 1749	£17 15s. 4d.		repairing road
	£20 0s. 0d.		bridge across Blackwater
31 May 1750		£10 5s. 5d.	repairing turnpike road
30 June 1750		£20 0s. 0d.	turnpike road
22 July 1750		£10 0s. 0d.	turnpike road
9 Aug. 1750	£15 3s. 4d.		two presentments of roads
13 Aug. 1750		£4 11s. 0d.	repairing turnpike work
23 May 1751		£10 0s. 0d.	turnpike road
Total	**£127 4s. 0d.**	**£72 3s. 7d.**	

Source: CTAB

local wealthy and interested landowners to improve the roads. By levying tolls on the road users, the roads and their upgrading and maintenance would be self-sufficient. The Navan–Kells turnpike road ran past the demesne house at Mount Tisdall and for a distance along the townlands of Martry and Hurdlestown, on the northern boundary of the Tisdall estate. Thomas Taylor, Lord Headfort, was a major stake-holder and a subscriber to this, one of the smaller turnpike trusts. Another trustee was Charles Hamilton of Dunboyne, executor of the Tisdall estate at the time. On 30 May 1738, Charles Hamilton directed Robert Waller, agent on the estate during Tisdall's minority, to invest £400 in the venture, from which Charles received regular interest money of £20 annually, indicating an interest rate of 5 per cent.[77] Investment in the turnpike road had a triple effect. It was potentially a profitable investment, generating much-needed supplementary income for the landlord, while improving the locality's infrastructure and providing employment for tenants and workers on the estate. In turn, this ensured extra income for tenants, independent of farming and its vagaries, which could pay their landlord's rents.

By the time Charles inherited his estate, both the Dublin–Navan and Navan–Kells turnpike roads had been completed and were gravelled and widened and the ditches deepened and drained. They had still to be maintained and repaired. At a meeting of 14 of the commissioners of the Navan-Kells turnpike trust on 1 October 1736, the management of the trust was put into the hands of Sir Thomas Taylor, Kells, the main stakeholder.[78] This arrangement later benefitted Charles, who was a near neighbour, a fellow member of the Meath grand jury and a friend of Thomas Taylor. Not only did Charles receive interest on his investment of £400, he also secured contracts for work on the turnpike road on eight occasions during the period under study, generating an income of £72 3s. 7d. (table 3.2). He appears to have carried out all the improving work on the stretches of the turnpike road that ran along his estate.

These infrastructural improvements shortened travelling time and cut transport costs for carriage of goods and personnel to and from the estate, a very important consideration for Charles who travelled frequently. Charles also levelled a steep hill on the road between Kells and Charlesfort House, moving tons of earth in the process, so that his horse could take the hill in a canter.[79] Charles regularly contributed towards the cleaning and 'scowering' of the rivers running through his estate, sharing the expenses of cleaning the river between 'Great Athgaine and Roodstown and the ditch joining Moyagher' with William Waller.[80] On 2 August 1745, Thomas Taylor and Charles made 321 perches of new river between their respective holdings at Ballybeg and Martry, costing each of them £24 1s. 6d. In 1749, Charles altered the course of the river at Nugentstown to 'make the mearing more straight'.[81] He also built a new avenue to his new demesne house, Charlesfort House.

LINEN INDUSTRY

Improving gentlemen were advised to establish manufactures on their lands, especially those of yarn and cloth and to distribute flax seed and lay out bleaching yards. Charles took this advice to heart and established 'the factory' on his estate in 1743.[82] Flax-growing and linen production had been carried on in Ireland from medieval times. When parliament placed a punitive levy on woollen exports from Ireland, a Board of Trustees of the Linen and Hempen Manufacturers of Ireland, known as The Linen Board, was formed in 1711 to promote the linen trade. It subsidized the purchase of spinning wheels and looms. Progressive landlords encouraged flax-growing and established mills and markets as a means to increase employment and prosperity on their estates. Flax growing and the linen industry were concentrated in Ulster in places such as the Abercorn and Downshire estates. Charles would have seen the success of the industry on his travels to Ulster, visiting relatives and friends where he met and socialized with other landlords experimenting with establishing a linen industry. His step-father, the Revd Dr Hudson, was from Omagh and was a confidant on church matters of the 8th earl of Abercorn, who had established a linen industry on his estate. His future

Table 3.3. The 'factory'

Date	Item	Cost
June 1743	20 spinning wheels, 4 reels, 2 looms	£5 11s. 0d.
Aug. 1743	screw pump 18 ft x 19 ins diameter and carriage	£12 19s. 10d.
	bleaching pan containing 100 gallons, grate, iron door	£6 11s. 0d.
	wages for working horse wheel to turn screw pump	£1 10s. 0d.
Nov. 1743	sentinel box for factory	£1 13s. 0d.
Feb. 1743/4	half barrel gunpowder	£2 5s. 0d.
May 1748	screw pump 24 feet long	£12 0s. 0d.
Total		**£42 9s. 10d.**

Source: CTAB

brother-in-law, Arthur Hamilton Maxwell, had established a bleaching mill in Drum in Co. Down.[83] Spinning and weaving were cottage industries among the tenants in Meath. The poet William Ó Maoilchiaráin lived in Oristown, close by the Tisdall estate and was a contemporary of Charles Tisdall.[84] William's wife Síghle used to spin and travelled to south Ulster on one occasion to buy 'tow', the cheapest part of scutched flax.[85] The linen industry, then, was an obvious activity to encourage and promote. It would also help his tenants to pay their rents.

Charles built a flax mill on the estate, which he always referred to as 'the factory', and started a fledgling flax industry. The factory was located close to two water-driven corn mills in Nugentstown.[86] In March 1743, the first purchase of flax seed is recorded (table 3.3). Charles paid 13s. 6d. for dressing 16 stone of flax seed at 10d. a stone.[87] In June he ordered 20 spinning wheels, four reels and two looms from the Linen Board costing £5 11s.[88] This represented half the cost of the goods. He was later reimbursed by the Linen Board.[89] In August he paid £12 19s. 10d. for a screw pump and invested £6 11s. in a beaching pan, a grate and an iron door. The pump was powered by the 'workmanship of a horse wheel'.[90] In November, a sentinel box was needed, which suggests that the factory was substantial and needed securing.[91] On 9 March 1743/4, he paid £6 11s. 6d. to the Linen Board for 6½ barrels of flax seed.[92] Fifty years later in 1796, the list of flax growers of Ireland recorded 12 flax growers in the civil parish of Martry on the Tisdall estate including John Murray, the tenant on the old demesne, Mount Tisdall.[93] The 1821 census returns also survive for the townland of Martry.[94] Out of a population of 139 adults, 27 were engaged in the linen industry as weavers or spinners almost 80 years after Charles made his first investment in the industry.[95] Jack Gaughran had a piece of linen in his possession which was made in 'the factory', the ruins of which were demolished in the 1940s.[96]

Table 3.4. Merchants used in building work and tree plantation

Name	Goods	Location
Mr Thompson	furniture supplier	Dublin
Mr Bonvillette	timber merchant	Dublin
Maurice Tyrrel	Ardbraccan stone	Ardbraccan
John Paine	trees	not stated
William Brabings	boards	not stated
Valentine Olgan	boards	not stated
George Clegg	glazing	Drogheda
Michael Quin	nursery	not stated
Ian Hatch	timber	Not stated
Oliver Crekan	trees	not stated
Michael Kinsella	nursery	not stated
George Stewart	sentinel box	not stated

Source: CTAB

MORAL IMPROVEMENT

Another aspect of the 'improving' culture of the period was to elevate not only the material, but the spiritual and cultural level of the people as well. Charles was an honorary member of the Incorporated Society for promoting English Protestant working schools in Ireland in 1751. Its members were a 'who's who' of Irish genteel society and included many of Charles' friends and fellow improvers.[97] The society opened a charter school for 40 pupils in Ardbraccan near Navan in Co. Meath in 1747.[98] Ardbraccan lay close to the new demesne house in Charlesfort that Charles was building and the family worshipped in Ardbraccan church when Charlesfort was completed. On 24 April 1751, Charles paid £2 14s. 11d. for half a seat in the church, 'next to the communion table'.[99]

Charter schools were seen as an 'agent of improvement' for Ireland's economic future and perceived as very much in keeping with the country's needs. Catholics were admitted on condition that they were educated as Protestants. Like the other charter schools, Ardbraccan focused on training girls for domestic service in the houses of the gentry and aristocracy, while training boys in agriculture and gardening. Charles' granduncle, Robert FitzGerald, 19th earl of Kildare, championed the charter school cause, donating the large sum of £500 towards the prototype school in Castledermot, Co. Kildare, erected in May 1734. An improving landlord like Charles Tisdall saw in the school a means to inculcate habits of good husbandry, while providing a ready supply of skilled protestant-educated workers for his estate.[100] Accordingly, on 3 May 1746 he donated

£11 7s. 6d. towards the cost of building the Richard Castle-designed school in Ardbraccan.[101] Regular subscribers were needed and Charles continued to support the school, paying an annual subscription of £1 9s. 3d. in 1750 and a similar amount again in 1751, the year that the account book ends.[102]

The society aimed to establish a school in each province which would then serve as a model to private schools. Perhaps Charles planned setting up his own private school on the estate. However, he died young, and it was his son, Michael IV, who established the estate school, called Charlesfort. It was still in operation in 1835, when the free school catered for 44 of the labourers' children. As well as teaching reading, writing, arithmetic and grammar, with needlework for the girls, scriptural instruction was included.[103] The school building no longer survives but the site is still remembered in the landscape today as 'the schoolhouse field'.

Charles also gave money towards rebuilding Protestant churches in the locality. His first charitable donation was in 1741 when he contributed 2s. 3d. towards church repairs in Kells.[104] In September 1744, he donated the much-larger sum of £4 17s. 9½d. towards 'the assembly' at Syddan in Co. Meath.[105] Charles owned considerable property in Drogheda and in January 1748/9, he gave £2 5s. 6d. towards the building of St Peter's Church, the earlier St Peter's Church had been burned down. The new church was designed by Hugh Darley, whose relative was Charles' stone mason, perhaps an extra incentive for Charles to donate.[106] Four months after his sister's marriage to Arthur Maxwell Hamilton of Drum in August 1750, Charles donated £3 7s. 6d. to Mr Mecom, the Presbyterian minister, towards building a meeting house at Drum, possibly at the request of his new brother-in-law.[107]

Charles Tisdall undertook all his improving work over an 11-year time span. His motives for the building work, tree plantation and building of the linen factory and subscription to the charter school may have been mixed. Perhaps he subscribed to the 'improving' ethos, believing that the best way to improve the fortune of the peasantry was to provide work for them.[108] Perhaps he wanted to set a standard for his tenants to imitate, by exposing them to new ideas. However, his motives may not have been entirely altruistic. Economy and financial security may have been an important factor. Whatever reasons he had for undertaking it, the results were the same. His 'improving' ethic boosted the economy, locally and even further afield (tables 3.1 and 3.4). His 'factory' provided work for tradesmen, weavers, mill workers and spinners, many of whom were his tenants. Payment of rents could be better ensured if families had the supplementary income from flax-growing and its related spin-offs of spinning and weaving. This in turn, guaranteed Charles' income too.

Conclusion

This study has added substance to the one-dimensional representation of Charles Tisdall in the Stephen Slaughter portrait and answers the question: who was the man in the painting? A modish young Protestant gentleman, he was the first resident Tisdall landlord on the Meath estate. This had a major, instant impact on the lives of his tenants and local community. When Charles took up residence in Mount Tisdall as the new landlord, he immediately needed a staff of domestic servants and workmen to run the household and the farm. This created employment, where none, or little, had existed previously. In an eight-year period, Charles' wages bill to these two staffs amounted to £3,257 3s. 5d.[1] It was a much-needed injection of money into the local economy, enabling tenants to pay their rents and purchase goods, which in turn stimulated further economic activity. Charles recognized the importance of the family's residence there. In his will, dated 1754, he recommended that his wife Hester, 'live at least one month yearly at my deer park' until their son was 21, and afterwards if she chose to build a house on the estate, he left her generous provisions.[2]

Central to the understanding of the personality of Charles Tisdall is the seemingly contradictory duality of his actions. The apparently self-centred, extravagant youth, revelling at home and on the Continent, dressing flamboyantly and travelling the country-side by French post-chaise, was, within two years of coming into his inheritance, actively engaged in improving his estate. After the initial spendthrift years, all of his energies seemed to have been invested in the estate. There was an almost-imperceptible character change from one role to the other. It was as though what Charles considered an appropriate lifestyle for a young man was not fitting for a landlord with responsibilities. Appearances decided ranking, so appearances mattered in the early uncertain years of his stewardship. Then when his ranking was established, he adopted the second precept that restraint, and conduct appropriate to one's station, was important.

In the early 1740s, Charles was engaged in a merry-go-round of travel at a time when travel was slow and difficult, yet this travel was to stand his estate and community in good stead in later years. It introduced Charles to wider perspectives and new ideas, through places visited and people met, ideas he later implemented on his own estate. It was the stimulus and springboard that informed his policy of improvement. His visits to England and the Continent kept him abreast of new trends, such as those in landscape design, where the shift was towards creating a romantic, pastoral scene, and away from earlier formal creations. His frequent trips north to visit relatives and friends surely influenced him in establishing the linen factory on his estate.

Charles embraced his responsibilities as landlord, and managed his estate by the tenet that his role was that of a caretaker for his tenants and future generations, feeling duty-bound to hand on his inheritance in a better condition than he received it.[3] 'All moveable stock and goods' were immediately sold when his father, Michael Tisdall III, died in 1726. The terms of his father's will left Charles with a large blank canvas of empty rolling fields.[4] There was no stock, few trees and fewer hedges. Charles was an able manager though, and by 1751 had transformed this canvas. The newly completed Charlesfort House and demesne, surrounded by thousands of young trees, dominated the landscape. The fields were stocked with sheep and cattle, the rivers with fish. Roads and bridges were improved. Mount Tisdall was repaired, labourers' cottages were built, the wheel at Martry Mill was turning again and a linen factory had been established. Activity on the estate may have engendered hope and excitement among the tenantry, together with the expectancy, perhaps, of brighter times ahead. The sight of so many workmen busily engaged in improving the estate in a short concentrated period of 11 years may have instilled optimism among the tenantry that the economy was at last in the ascendant. Perhaps it promoted a sense of pride too.

Charles was an improving landlord, believing that the proper care of his inheritance meant more than 'maximizing its revenues'.[5] There were other like-minded contemporaries, such as Robert French of Monivea (1716–79). But what made Charles unique was that, though a landlord of a modest estate, he was an early forerunner of the 'improving' movement. He was ahead of his time. Charles began work on the linen factory in 1743, Robert French not until 1747.[6] Charlesfort House was built 1742–51, Thomas Taylor, owner of 21,000 acres nearby, did not commence building Headfort House until 1751.[7] Where to place Charles Tisdall and his estate in the national context of what was happening in mid-18th century Ireland presents a quandary. Charles was not a figure on the national stage. He was neither titled nor a member of parliament. Although he rubbed shoulders with the great and the good, he was a middling-sized country landowner of the gentry class. He lived a less extravagant version of the life of his cousin the duke of Leinster. He had some of the trappings of his wealthier relative, but on a lesser scale. He built a Richard Castle-designed house, but a smaller one, he bought silver from the same silversmith, but less of it. He entertained well but not as lavishly. Charles lived on an estate of less than 3,000 acres. However, he travelled extensively on the Grand Tour and dressed like a 'grand figure'.

A consideration of just three aspects of his life, his material world, the management structure he established on his Meath estate and the improving work he initiated there, suggests that he fits into a pattern identified by other historians of the 18th-century élite. He occupied a middle position: somewhat lower than the aristocracy, but higher than the large tenant farmer. Charles died young at the age of 37 in 1757. Who knows what he might have accomplished had he lived to a ripe old age?

Notes

ABBREVIATIONS

BIGS	Bulletin of the Irish Georgian Society
CTAB	Charles Tisdall's account book, 1740–51
DD	Dublin Directory
DEP	Dublin Evening Post
DPJ	Dublin Penny Journal
FDJ	Faulkner's Dublin Journal
GO	Genealogical Office
HC	House of Commons
NAI	National Archives of Ireland
NLI	National Library of Ireland
OS	Ordnance Survey
PRONI	Public Record Office, Northern Ireland
RD	Registry of Deeds
RWAB	Robert Waller's account book, 1727–40

Note on dating: Until 1752, the year began on 25 March (Lady Day) in Britain and Ireland (old style) but from 1582 for most of Europe the year began on 1 January (new style), so dating for this study, 1740–51, is according to both styles. Dating is according to old style for the day and the month, but new style for the year, e.g., 24 March 1741/2 but 25 March 1742.

INTRODUCTION

1 Interview with Anthony Tisdall, Ascot, Berkshire, England, 14 Sept. 2012.
2 Bernard Burke, *Burke's Irish family records* (London, 1976), pp 1104–9.
3 Books of Survey and Distribution, County Eastmeath (NLI, MS 974); R.C. Simington (ed.), *The Civil Survey, A.D. 1654–1656: County of Meath* (Dublin, 1940), v.
4 Joseph Byrne, *Byrne's dictionary of Irish local history from earliest times to c.1900* (Dublin, 2004), p. 96.
5 The Civil Survey (NLI, MS 974), p. 72.
6 Fine between Michael Tisdall gent, plaintiff, Nicholas Darcy and Catherine, his wife, deforciants: of the manor of Martry, 1669, transcribed in John Ainsworth (ed.), 'Report on private collections, Tisdall Papers (from 1630)', (NLI, Report no. 290).
7 NLI, MS 974, p. 72.
8 Charles Tisdall's account book, 1740–51 (hereinafter referred to as CTAB; MS in the possession of Anthony Tisdall, Ascot, Berkshire, England).
9 Charlesfort House is 230 ft above sea level; Paddy Kerrigan concurs that Bloomsbury House, alias Bloomsberry House, alias Mount Tisdall, was very damp. On renovating it in 2010, he spent days pumping water from the basement, even though the water level of the river is lower now than in the 1740s, the river having been dredged in the 1970s.
10 CTAB, 7 Aug., 28 Oct. 1740; the brewery was leased to Patrick Sweetman, brewer, for half-yearly rent of £24.
11 Tony Coogan and Jack Gaughran, *Charlesfort: the story of a Meath estate and its people, 1668–1968* (Navan, 1991).
12 Anthony Doyle, *Charles Powell Leslie II's estates at Glaslough, County Monaghan, 1800–41* (Dublin, 2001).

13 Denis A. Cronin, *A Galway gentleman in the age of improvement: Robert French of Monivea, 1716–79* (Dublin, 1995).

14 William H. Crawford, *The management of a major Ulster estate in the late eighteenth century: the eighth earl of Abercorn and his Irish agents* (Dublin, 2001).

15 Joe Clarke, *Christopher Bellew and his Galway estates, 1763–1826* (Dublin, 2003).

16 Terence Dooley, *The big houses and landed estates of Ireland: a resource guide* (Dublin, 2008), p. 66.

17 Ainsworth (ed.), 'Report on private collections, the Tisdall Papers', (NLI); John Ainsworth visited Charlesfort in the 1950s and surveyed the material held there in Dr O.R. Tisdall's private possession; in 1968, the house and estate were sold and the family moved to England, when some family papers were lost.

18 CTAB, 1 Apr. 1740 to 29 July 1751.

19 Personal accounts of Richard Edgeworth, of Edgeworthstown, Jan. 1759–July 1770 (NLI, MSS 1525–36); two account books of Richard Edgeworth, papers of the Edgeworth family, 1727–1894 (Longford County Library); copy of diary of John Pratt of Agher, Co. Meath, Sept. 1745 to May 1747, with genealogical notes on the Pratt family, 1711–61 (NLI, microfilm, p. 4160).

20 Marie-Louise Legg (ed.), *The diary of Nicholas Peacock, 1740–1751* (Dublin, 2005).

21 Reminiscences of Christie Ward, Tisdall Papers (NLI, microfilm, p. 4692); *DEP*, 2–6 Jan. 1739–40; see David Dickson, *Arctic Ireland: the extraordinary frost and forgotten famine of 1740–41* (2nd ed., Belfast, 1998).

22 CTAB, 1 Apr. 1740 to 29 July 1751; for Stephen Slaughter see Walter Strickland, *A dictionary of Irish artists* (2 vols, Dublin and London, 1913), ii, 359.

23 See Edith Mary Johnston-Liik, *History of the Irish Parliament* (6 vols, Belfast, 2002), vi, 405–8.

24 Barnard, *Making the grand figure*, p. xx.

25 Interview with Anthony Tisdall, 14 Sept. 2012.

26 CTAB, 1 Apr. 1740 to 29 July 1751.

27 Robert Waller, agent's account book 1727–40, (hereinafter referred to as RWAB, MS in the possession of Anthony Tisdall).

28 Reminiscences of Christie Ward, Tisdall Papers (NLI, microfilm, p. 4692).

29 Rent roll and list of securities of Michael Tisdall (NLI, microfilm, p. 4692).

30 Instructions for preparing flax, Tisdall Papers (NLI, microfilm, p. 4692).

31 K.H. Connell, 'The land legislation and Irish social life' *Economic History Review*, n.s., 11:1 (1958), 2–7.

32 Kells turnpike journal (NLI, Headfort papers, MS 25,450); CTAB, 7 Aug., 28 Oct. 1740.

33 Religious census, 1766 (GO, MS 537).

34 The census of Ireland for the year 1821, Martry parish in County Meath (NAI microfilm copy in Meath County Library, Navan).

35 CTAB, 29 Aug., 8 Oct., 4 Nov., 16 Nov. 1743.

36 Irish flax growers 1796 (http://www.failteromhat.com/flax1796.php) (accessed 16 April 2012).

37 CTAB, 13 Aug. 1743.

1. THE MATERIAL WORLD OF CHARLES TISDALL

1 Toby Barnard, *A new anatomy of Ireland: the Irish Protestants, 1649–1770* (London, 2003), p. 18.

2 Phrase used by Toby Barnard for title of book, *Making the grand figure*.

3 Burke, *Burke's records*, pp 1104–9; Mary Johnston-Liik (ed.), *History of the Irish parliament, 1692–1800* (6 vols, Belfast, 2007), vi, 405–8.

4 CTAB, 1 Apr. 1740–29 July 1751.

5 See Dickson, *Arctic Ireland*, pp 11–57.

6 CTAB, 1740–51.

7 Burke, *Burke's records*, p. 1106; see Johnston-Liik, *History of the Irish parliament*, vi, 404.

8 Ainsworth (ed.), 'Report on private collections, the Tisdall Papers'.

9 Burke, *Burke's records*, pp 1106; George James Burtchaell and Thomas Ulick Sadleir (eds), *Alumni Dublinenses, 1593–1860* (3 vols, Bristol, 2001), iii, 813.

10 CTAB, 2 Feb. 1740/1.

11 CTAB, 15 Jan. 1742/3; William Napper, Loughcrew, Oldcastle, son of James Napper, High Sheriff of Meath, 1701.

12 Prerogative will of Michael Tisdall, Mount Tisdall, Co. Meath, 25 Jan. 1724/5 proved 12 Feb. 1727/8 (NAI on microfilm, MFGS 41/3); RWAB.

13 CTAB, 24 Dec. 1745; RWAB, May 1736.

14 See Cynthia O'Connor, *The pleasing hours: James Caulfeild, first earl of Charlemont, 1728–99: traveller, connoisseur* (Cork, 1999); Elizabeth FitzGerald, *Lord Kildare's grand tour: the letters of William Fitzgerald, 1766–69* (Cork, 2000).

15 CTAB, Sept. 1739 to Apr. 1740; RWAB, 5 Oct., 10 Oct. 1739.

16 Charles Tisdall spelled it Swadlingbar; Swanlinbar is the current spelling of the town and will be used hereinafter.

17 CTAB, abstract Dec. 1744.

18 Constantia Maxwell, *Country and town in Ireland under the Georges* (London, 1940, revised ed., Dundalk, 1949), p. 278.

19 CTAB, 28 May 1741; they were celebrating the vice-admiral's victory, even though he had departed, defeated, after 67 days' battle, from Carthagena for Jamaica 20 May 1741, having suffered one of the worst naval defeats in history – King George II never allowed details of the defeat to be published so he was welcomed back to England as a hero, commemorative victory coins were minted.

20 CTAB, 25 Apr. 1746; See James Kelly and Martyn J. Powell (eds), *Clubs and societies in eighteenth-century Ireland* (Dublin, 2010); Maxwell, *Ireland under the Georges*, p. 21.

21 CTAB, Aug. 1741, 18 Oct. 1746.

22 Letter from Thomas Taylor to Thomas Taylor, Headfort, Kells, 30 July 1749 (NLI, MS 48, 880/2).

23 Richard Twiss, *A tour in Ireland in 1775 with a map and a view of the Salmon Leap at Ballyshannon* (London, 1776), p. 107.

24 Isaac Butler's journey: itinerary of a journey through Counties Dublin, Meath, Louth containing drawings [etc.] (NLI, microfilm, p. 6486).

25 CTAB, 21 Aug. 1741, the six, who contributed a moydore each, were Colonel Hugh Willoughby, Cosby Nesbitt, Benjamin Copeland, Charles Eccles, Major Carmichael and Henry Cunningham.

26 John Rutty, *Essay towards natural and experimental and medicinal history of the mineral waters of Ireland* (Dublin, 1757), pp 362–407.

27 CTAB, 27 Aug. 1745, 26 Aug. 1747.

28 CTAB, 12 Aug. 1741.

29 RWAB, 13 May 1727.

30 CTAB, 11 Jan. 1744/5; L.M. Cullen, 'Economic development, 1691–1750' in T.W. Moody and W.E. Vaughan (eds), *A new history of Ireland*, iv: *eighteenth-century Ireland, 1691–1800* (Oxford, 1986), p. 146.

31 CTAB, 4 June 1747, 12 Jan. 1741/2, 31 Oct. 1743, 26 June 1745, 11 Jan. 1745/6, 29 Mar. 1748.

32 CTAB, 14 May 1741.

33 CTAB, 7 Mar. 1744/5.

34 CTAB, 15 Oct. 1744, 11 Jan. 1745/6, 20 Feb. 1745/6.

35 CTAB, 30 Nov. 1745.

36 CTAB, Oct. 1741.

37 CTAB, 1 Oct. 1741.

38 Copy of grant of arms to Michael Tisdall, J.P. 1679 (NLI, Tisdall papers on microfilm, p. 4692).

39 CTAB, 5 Oct. 1741; for Drogheda damask, see James Kelly (ed.), *The letters of Lord Chief Baron Edward Willes to the earl of Warwick, 1757–62: an account of Ireland mid-eighteenth* (Aberystwyth, 1990), p. 28.

40 CTAB, 13 Jan. 1741/2.

41 Interview with Tony Coogan of Navan, June 2012.

42 Barnard, *Making the grand figure*, pp 251–3.

43 CTAB, 20 Sept. 1741.

44 CTAB, 1 Oct., 5 Oct. 1741.

45 CTAB, 2 Nov. 1741.

46 CTAB, 19 Nov. 1741.

47 CTAB, 18 June 1746.

48 CTAB; RD, 107/ 429/ 74803.

49 CTAB, 16 July 1744, 27 June 1745.

50 CTAB, 2 Nov. 1745.

51 CTAB, 18 Jan. 1746/7.

52 CTAB, 27 June 1745.

53 CTAB, 20 Apr. 1744; accoutrements denote military equipment other than weapons and garments.

54 Noel Ross and Brendan Hall, 'The array of the militia in County Louth in 1745', *Co. Louth Archaeological and Historical Journal*, 24:3 (1999), 391–406.

55 Nicholas Peacock, journal, 24, 25 Nov. 1745 (NLI, MS 16,091).

56 NLI, microfilm, p. 4160.

57 *A list of officers in the several regiments and independent troops and companies of militia in*

Ireland (Dublin, 1761), pp 95–7 (Armagh Public Library, POO 1340812).

58 Ibid.

59 Barnard, *A new anatomy of Ireland*, p. 47.

60 For associational life, see Kelly and Powell (eds), *Clubs and societies*.

61 James Kelly, *The pastime of the élite: clubs and societies and the promotion of horse racing* (Dublin, 2010).

62 CTAB, 23 June 1741, 19 Dec. 1741; for horse-racing before 1800, see S.J. Watson, *Between the flags: a history of Irish steeplechasing* (Dublin, 1969), pp 1–30.

63 John Cheney, *Cheney's racing calendar* (London, 1727–50) cited in S.J. Watson, *Between the flags*, p. 14.

64 CTAB, 15 Aug. 1744, 10 Apr. 1741, 6 Dec. 1742.

65 John James McGregor, *New picture of Dublin: comprehending a history of the city; an accurate account of its various establishments and institutions, etc.* (London, 1821), p. 319; Joseph Archer, *Statistical survey of the county Dublin* (Dublin, 1801), p. 96.

66 CTAB, 2 Mar. 1740/1.

67 CTAB, 23 June 1741; this inn may have been Rochestown, Co. Dublin, frequented by those wishing to partake of goat's whey drink.

68 CTAB, June 1741, 30 Apr. 1741.

69 Lord Offaly until 1744, later duke of Leinster, married Lady Emily Lennox, 7 Feb. 1747; see Charles William Fitzgerald, *The earls of Kildare, and their ancestors: from 1057 to 1773* (Dublin, 1858).

70 Maxwell, *Ireland under the Georges*, pp 36–8; Mervyn Busteed, *Castle Caldwell, County Fermanagh: life on an Ulster estate, 1750–1800* (Dublin, 2006).

71 CTAB, 5 Oct. 1741, 9 June 1744.

72 No longer suitable as a boathouse since the level of the River Blackwater was lowered in the 1970s.

73 CTAB, 16 Aug. 1744, 27 Sept. 1746.

74 CTAB, 6 July, 24 Aug. 1742, 23 Sept, 8 Nov. 1746.

75 CTAB, 8 Nov. 1746, 24 Apr. 1750, 7 June 1751, 29 Sept. 1751.

76 CTAB, 7 June 1749.

77 CTAB, 2 Mar. 1741/2, 25 Mar. 1742.

78 CTAB, 20 Sept. 1741, 15 Sept. 1744, 7 Dec. 1744.

79 Barnard, *A new anatomy of Ireland*, p. 43.

80 CTAB, 5 Oct. 1741.

81 CTAB, 21 Nov. 1747; perhaps it was on Oxmantown Green, Dublin.

82 Brian Boydell, *A Dublin musical calendar, 1700–1760* (Dublin, 1988), p.12.

83 CTAB, 2 Feb. 1740/1; for music, see Brian Boydell, 'Music before 1700' in Moody and Vaughan (eds), *A new history of Ireland*, iv, pp 542–628; William H. Grattan Flood, *A history of Irish music* (Dublin, 1906), pp 243–313.

84 CTAB, 10 April 1750.

85 CTAB, 5 May 1742.

86 CTAB, 5 Dec. 1741; see Kelly and Powell (eds), *Clubs and societies*, pp 47–9; William H. Grattan Flood, *A history of Irish music*.

87 NLI, microfilm, p. 4160, p. 37.

88 *FDJ*, 9–12 Jan. 1741/2.

89 G.F. Handel, *Messiah, an oratorio* (London, 1741).

90 CTAB, 14 Feb. 1742/3, 27 Nov. 1743; for Dr Thomas Arne and Mrs Arne's concerts, see Boydell, 'Music 1700–1850', pp 591–2, 601–2, 622, 624; W.H. Grattan Flood, 'Fishamble St. Music Hall, Dublin, from 1741–1777', *Sammelbände der Internationalen Musikgesellschaft*, i (1912), 51–7.

91 CTAB, 6 Dec. 1742; for music hall in Crowe Street see Irish excavation reports (http://www.excavations.ie/Pages/Details.php?Year=&County=Dublin&id=183) (accessed 12 Nov. 2012).

92 CTAB, 6 May 1750; Burke, *Burke's records*, p. 1106.

93 CTAB, 30 Jan. 1740/1.

94 Raymond Gillespie and Andrew Hadfield (eds), *The Oxford history of the Irish book, vol. iii: The Irish book in English, 1550–1800* (Oxford, 2006), p. 151.

95 CTAB, 23 Dec. 1744, 24 Feb. 1744/5.

96 CTAB, 17 Dec. 1741.

97 CTAB, 21 Sept. 1742.

98 CTAB, 5 May 1747.

99 CTAB, 9 Feb. 1742/3.

100 CTAB, 28 Feb. 1740/1, 28 Mar. 1741.

101 CTAB, 9 June 1751.

102 Francis Elrington Ball, 'Stillorgan Park and its history', *Journal of the Royal Society of Antiquaries of Ireland*, 8 (1898), 21–34.

103 CTAB, 18 Jan. 1746/7; *Watson's almanac, 1746*, p. 70.

104 A hogshead was a favourite measure for claret, equalling 46 imperial gallons or 207 litres.
105 CTAB, 17 Oct. 1744.
106 CTAB, 4 Oct., 13 Oct., 19 Oct., 31 Oct. 1744.
107 CTAB, 15 Apr. 1746.
108 CTAB, 25 Mar. 1741, 30 May 1742.
109 CTAB, 20 Jan. 1741/2.
110 CTAB, 1 Oct., 3 Nov. 1741.
111 CTAB, 4 Feb. 1742/3.
112 CTAB, 1 Feb. 1743/4.
113 CTAB, 7 Dec. 1741 to 18 June 1750.
114 For silver purchased during this period by Charles' relatives, the earls of Kildare, see Joseph McDonnell, 'Irish rococo silver', *Irish Arts Review Yearbook*, 13 (1997), 78–87; Elsie Taylor, 'Silver for a countess's levee: the Kildare toilet service', *Irish Arts Review Yearbook*, 14 (1998), 115–24.
115 Reminiscences of Christie Ward (NLI, microfilm, p. 4692).
116 CTAB, 19 Dec. 1741; Barnard, *Making the grand figure*, p. 16.
117 McDonnell, 'Irish rococo silver', 78–87.
118 CTAB, 28 Feb. 1743/4.
119 CTAB, 3 July 1743.
120 CTAB, 19 July 1745.
121 CTAB, 15 Dec. 1741.
122 CTAB, 15 Apr. 1743.
123 CTAB, 27 Mar., 30 Oct. 1746.
124 CTAB, 15 July 1751.
125 CTAB, 29 May 1745.
126 Interview with Anthony Tisdall, Ascot, 14 Sept. 2012.
127 CTAB, 2 Oct. 1741.
128 Inscription on presentation box, courtesy Anthony Tisdall.
129 CTAB, 6 Dec. 1742.
130 See Strickland, *A dictionary of Irish artists*, ii, 359.
131 Barnard, *Making the grand figure*, p. 151.
132 CTAB, 1 Feb. 1748/9.
133 CTAB, 29 June 1750.
134 Burke, *Burke's records*, p. 1106.
135 Inscription on Charles Tisdall's memorial plaque on wall of Martry Church, Kells.

2. THE WORLD OF THE TISDALL ESTATE

1 Edith Mary Johnston, *Ireland in the eighteenth century* (Dublin, 1974), p. 1.

2 Fine between George Taafe, Dublin, gent, and Charles Tisdall esq., deforciant: 14 Geo. II 1741, transcribed in Ainsworth (ed.), 'Ainsworth report on private collections'.
3 CTAB, 11 Mar. 1745/6, 12 Apr. 1746. Charles' grandfather was married to Anne Barry, daughter of William Barry, rector of Killucan, Co. Meath, and niece of James Barry (1603–71), Lord Santry, 1661.
4 Terence Dooley, *The big houses and landed estates of Ireland: a research guide* (Dublin, 2000), p.18.
5 See pp 44–6 below.
6 Note in RWAB.
7 CTAB, observation by Charles included in abstract of value of lands held by him, May 1740–May 1746.
8 CTAB, abstract of disbursements 1744 including townlands and acreage in Charles' hands.
9 CTAB, 4 June 1741.
10 CTAB, 1 Apr. 1740–29 July 1751.
11 CTAB, 21 Aug. 1741.
12 CTAB, 28 May 1743.
13 RWAB, 1739.
14 Prerogative will of Michael Tisdall of Mount Tisdall, County Meath, 25 Jan. 1724/5 (NAI, microfilm, MFGS 41/3).
15 William Palmer was MP for Kildare 1695 and Castlebar 1723, see Burke, *Burke's records*, p. 1105.
16 For role of serjeantcy see J.L. McCracken, 'The political structure, 1714–60' in Moody and Vaughan (eds), *A new history of Ireland*, iv (1986), pp 57–83.
17 Speaker Boyle to Devonshire, recommending Serjeant Philip Tisdall for the prime serjeantcy, 6 Nov. 1742 (PRONI, T3158/232); Pedigree of Tisdall of Mount Tisdall, Charlesfort, Bawn, Teltown and Carrickfergus (PRONI, T883/1); Burke, *Burke's records*, p. 1104; letter to editor reminiscing about great lawyers of past including Philip Tisdall in *DPJ*, 27 Oct. 1832; portrait of Philip Tisdall in common room, Trinity College; Ball, 'Stillorgan Park', pp 21–34.
18 Headfort papers, Nobber turnpike journal (NLI, MS 25,451, 27 Aug. 1734, p. 6).
19 CTAB, July 1742–3, 30 June 1744.

20 RWAB; CTAB, 25 Mar. 1745.
21 Letter transcribed in Ainsworth (ed.),
'Ainsworth report on private collections',
a mearing is an unploughed strip
dividing open-field agricultural land
with perhaps temporary fencing.
22 CTAB, 26 Dec. 1743.
23 CTAB, in sundry payments 1751.
24 CTAB, 17 Apr. 1744; *DPJ*, 24 Apr. 1744.
25 For land and people in Meath, see Peter
Connell, *The land and people of County
Meath, 1750–1850* (Dublin, 2004).
26 RD, 143/373/97381.
27 CTAB, 28 Feb. 1744/5; Lewis Galliardy,
instituted rector and vicar of
Ardbraccan, and rector of Liscartan in
the county of Meath, 6 Mar. 1741, *The
London Magazine, or, Gentleman's Monthly
Intelligencer* (London, 1751).
28 CTAB, 8 May 1745.
29 CTAB, 27 Jan. 1743/4, 17 Apr. 1744;
DPJ, 24 Apr. 1744.
30 Cronin, *A Galway gentleman in the age of
improvement*, p. 17.
31 Reminiscences of Christie Ward (NLI,
microfilm, p. 4692); *DEP*, 2–6 Jan.
1739/40; L.M. Cullen, *An economic history
of Ireland since 1660* (London, 1972), pp
68–9; for more on climatic conditions see
Dickson, *Arctic Ireland*.
32 CTAB, 17 Apr. 1744, 25 Nov. 1747; *DJP*,
24 Apr. 1744.
33 CTAB, 4 June 1751.
34 Religious census, 1766 (GO MS 537);
RD 123/473/85411.
35 RWAB, 29 Mar. 1729.
36 RWAB, 1729, 1733.
37 CTAB, 2 May 1741.
38 CTAB, 23 Mar. 1740/1.
39 CTAB, 11 Mar. 1745/6.
40 OS Map 6", Meath, 17 (1836), copy in
Meath County Library, Navan.
41 CTAB, 9 July 1745.
42 CTAB, 7 Jan. 1748.
43 CTAB, 9 July 1745.
44 CTAB, 27 Feb. 1743/4, 27 June 1744, 30
Nov. 1744.
45 CTAB, 30 July 1742, 21 Apr. 1744.
46 CTAB, Aug. 1747.
47 CTAB, 2 Sept., 20 Sept., 6 Oct., 15 Oct.
1740, 27 Nov. 1741.
48 CTAB, 1743–51.
49 RWAB.
50 CTAB, penultimate page.

51 CTAB, 23 Mar. 1740/1.
52 CTAB, 24 Nov. 1743.
53 CTAB, 28 Feb. 1744/5.
54 Inscription on wall of Martry Mill,
courtesy of present owner, James Tallon.
55 CTAB, 28 July 1751.

3. AN IMPROVING LANDLORD

1 B.J. Graham (ed.), *A historical geography of
Ireland* (London, 1993), p. 227; for
'improvement', see Toby Barnard,
Improving Ireland? (Dublin, 2008), p. 64.
2 Graham (ed.), *Historical geography*, p. 227.
3 D.W. Hayton, 'Thomas Prior, Sir John
Rawdon, third baronet, and the
mentality and ideology of
"improvement": a question of
upbringing' in R. Gillespie and R.F.
Foster (eds), *Irish provincial cultures in the
long eighteenth century: essays for Toby
Barnard* (Dublin, 2013), p. 107.
4 David Dickson, *New foundations: Ireland
1660–1800* (Dublin, 1987), pp 108–9.
5 Letter from George Sackville, Knole to
Wilmot, 20 Oct. 1752 (PRONI, Wilmot
papers, T3019/1988) saying that if he
(Charles) would serve the government
his rank and his prosperity would entitle
him to the greatest favours from the lord
lieutenant (Lionel Sackville, the writer's
father).
6 For building activities of landlords, see
Dickson, *New foundations*, pp 108–9.
7 CTAB, 21 Sept. 1742.
8 Edward Malins and Knight of Glin, *Lost
demesnes: Irish landscape gardening 1660–
1845* (London, 1976).
9 CTAB, 24 Apr. 1751.
10 CTAB, 20 Aug. 1743; for Richard
Castle, see Christine Casey and Alistair
Rowan, *The buildings of Ireland: north
Leinster* (London, 1993), pp 43–4.
11 Notebook of Dr Oliver Raphael Tisdall
(1899–1964) in private ownership of his
son, Anthony Tisdall.
12 CTAB, 15 Apr. 1742.
13 CTAB, 20 Mar. 1742/3.
14 CTAB, 24 Dec. 1742.
15 Compiled from CTAB, Apr. 1742–Dec.
1742.
16 CTAB, 29 June 1742.
17 Maxwell, *Ireland under the Georges*, p. 189.
18 Dickson, *New foundations*, pp 108–9.

19 For Ardbraccan quarry, see Tony Hand, 'The white quarry, Ardbraccan', *Irish Architectural and Decorative Studies*, 8 (2005), 139–59.
20 RD, 123/ 473/ 85511.
21 CTAB, 1 Mar. 1743/4.
22 CTAB, 19 Sept. 1749.
23 CTAB, June 1746 to Apr. 1748.
24 CTAB, 26 June 1746, 24 Aug. 1748, 13 Oct. 1748.
25 CTAB, 12 Apr. 1748.
26 CTAB, 11 Sept. 1746.
27 CTAB, 29 Oct. 1747.
28 CTAB, 27 Oct. 1746.
29 CTAB, 7 Nov. 1746.
30 CTAB, 4 Jan. 1747/8.
31 *Dictionary of Irish architects, 1720–1940* (http://www.dia.ie/architects/view/1393 /DARLEY-HENRY%5B2%5D*) (accessed 8 Nov. 2012).
32 CTAB, 21 Nov. 1743.
33 CTAB, 23 Dec. 1744.
34 Lease Tisdall to Waller, RD, 150/ 162/ 10068.
35 RWAB, 1728.
36 CTAB, 28 Feb. 1740/1; pointing is an expensive and labour intensive process of renewing external part of mortar joints in masonry to prevent water entering, done about once every hundred years.
37 CTAB, 27 Nov. 1741.
38 CTAB, 28 Feb. 1743/4.
39 CTAB, 7 June 1751.
40 CTAB, 30 Jan. 1743/4.
41 CTAB, 16 Oct. 1749.
42 CTAB, 12 June 1749.
43 CTAB, 16 Oct. 1749.
44 CTAB, 11 July 1749.
45 CTAB, 27 May 1745, 28 July 1750.
46 CTAB, 24 Feb. 1743/4.
47 CTAB, 16 Dec. 1746.
48 CTAB, 19 Feb. 1747/8.
49 CTAB, 5 May 1747.
50 CTAB, 10 Sept. 1748.
51 CTAB, 27 Jan. 1747/8.
52 See James Howley, *The follies and garden buildings of Ireland* (London, 1993); Patricia Friel, *Frederick Trench (1746–1936) and Heywood, Queen's County: the creation of a romantic demesne* (Dublin, 2000); Robert Jocelyn, earl of Roden, *Tollymore: The story of an Irish demesne* (Belfast, 2005).
53 CTAB, 29 Sept. 1748.
54 CTAB, 12 Apr. 1748; book containing records of courts leet and courts baron held in the manor of Martry, Co. Meath, 1789–92 (NLI, microfilm, p. 4692).
55 CTAB, 29 Sept. 1748.
56 CTAB, 25 May 1744.
57 CTAB, 25 Dec. 1748.
58 CTAB, 20 June 1744.
59 Casey and Rowan, *The buildings of north Leinster*, p. 227.
60 Dickson, *Arctic Ireland*, p. 15.
61 Thomas Kinsella (ed.), *An duanaire, 1600–1900, poems of the dispossessed* (Dublin, 1981), p. 328.
62 Fine between George Taafe, and Charles Tisdall, Ainsworth (ed.), 'Ainsworth report on private collections'; CTAB, 16 Feb. 1748/9.
63 See J.L. McCracken, 'The social structure and social life, 1714–60' in Moody and Vaughan (eds), *A new history of Ireland*, iv, pp 31–56.
64 Taken from Austin Clarke's 'The Planter's Daughter'.
65 CTAB, 27 Aug. 1748.
66 CTAB, 23 Mar. 1748/9.
67 CTAB, 1 Apr. 1749.
68 CTAB, 28 Nov. 1744; quicks are young plants used in hedging; native wild crab apple trees are colourful seasonal provider of flower and fruit.
69 CTAB, 22 Jan. 1740/1; John Barrell, *The idea of landscape and the sense of place* (Cambridge, 1972), p. 5.
70 NLI, microfilm, p. 4160, p. 39, other members attending on 3 Mar. 1745/6 with John Pratt were: William Rawdon, High Sheriff, Sir Thomas Taylor, R. Westley, H. Rowley, N. Preston, B. Worthington, Charles Hamilton, George Lowther, R. Percevall, Benjamin Pratt, Bob Percevall, Charles Tisdall, M. Crofton, B. Copeland, Waller, J. Ashe, B. Woodward, Chaloner, J. Pepper, C. Fortescue, Somerville, G. Nugent, Towler, O Moore, judges, C. B. Bowes and J. Ward.
71 Subscribers' list for a county map of Meath, Representative Church Body Library, D/7/12/1/4.
72 CTAB, 5 Sept. 1749.
73 CTAB, 7 June 1751.
74 CTAB, 14 Apr. 1743.
75 CTAB, 1 Nov. 1748.

76 9 Anne c. 9 s. 9.
77 RWAB, 30 May/June 1738.
78 Headfort papers, Navan–Kells turnpike road minutes (NLI, MS 25,450, 1 Oct. 1736, p. 27).
79 Interview with Anthony Tisdall, Ascot, 14 Sept. 2012.
80 CTAB, 20 June 1748.
81 CTAB, 28 July 1749.
82 For the history of the Clark family and the Ulster linen trade, 1700–60, see Wallace Clark, *Linen on the green* (2nd ed. Belfast, 1983), pp 1–24.
83 Walter Harris, *The ancient and present state of the county of Down: containing a chorographical description with the natural and civil history of the same* (Dublin, 1744).
84 Énrí Ó Muirgheasa (ed.), *Amhráin na Midhe* (Dublin and Cork, 1934), pp 15–57, 171–4; William died in 1766.
85 William berated her for deserting him in a dialogue 'Uilliam 'Aol Chiaráin agus a bhean Síghle'; see Ó Muirgheasa (ed.), *Amhráin na Midhe*, p. 21.
86 OS Map, 1:10, 560, Meath, sheet 17, (1836), (Meath County Library, Navan).
87 CTAB, 28 Mar. 1743; seed dressing refers to the process of removing chaff, weed seeds and straw from the seed.
88 CTAB, 5 June 1743.
89 CTAB, 4 June 1743; for the Linen Board, see L.M. Cullen, 'Economic development, 1691–1750' in Moody and Vaughan (eds), *A new history of Ireland*, iv, pp 123–95.
90 CTAB, Aug. 1743.
91 CTAB, 16 Nov. 1743.
92 CTAB, 9 May 1744.
93 Irish flax growers 1796 (http://www.failteromhat.com/flax1796.php) (accessed 16 Apr. 2012).
94 1821 census, Martry, on microfilm in Navan Library.
95 Conrad Gill, *The rise of the Irish linen industry* (Oxford, 1925).
96 Tony Coogan saw this piece of linen in 1960s.

97 Subscription list 31 Dec. 1751, *A list of the honorary members of the Incorporated Society in Dublin, for promoting English Protestant working schools in Ireland.*
98 Kenneth Milne, *The Irish charter schools, 1730–1830* (Dublin, 1997), pp 55–6.
99 CTAB, 24 Apr. 1751.
100 Milne, *Irish charter schools*, pp 12–24.
101 CTAB, 3 May 1746; Milne, *Irish charter schools*; Kenneth Milne, 'Irish charter schools', *Irish Journal of Education/ Iris Éireannach an Oideachais*, 8 (1974), 3–29; The Knight of Glin, 'Richard Castle, architect, his biography and works', *Bulletin of the Irish Georgian Society*, 7.1 (Jan.–Mar. 1964), 31–38.
102 CTAB, 3 July 1750, 28 July 1751.
103 *First report of the commissioners of public instruction, Ireland*, HC 1835 [45] [46] [47], xxxiii.1, 829, xxxiv.1, 141.
104 CTAB, 28 May 1741.
105 CTAB, 11 Sept. 1744.
106 Casey and Rowan, *The buildings of north Leinster*, pp 237–8; CTAB, 27 Jan. 1748/9.
107 CTAB, 4 Aug. 1750.
108 Maxwell, *Ireland under the Georges*, p. 189.

CONCLUSION

1 CTAB, end of year abstract of yearly wages to domestic staff and workmen 1741–9, 1748 is missing.
2 Abstract of will of Charles Tisdall 1754 in John Ainsworth (ed.), 'Report on private collections, the Tisdall Papers' (NLI), pp 2267–8.
3 See Barnard, *A new anatomy of Ireland*, pp 41–80.
4 Will of Michael Tisdall (NAI, microfilm, MFGS 41/3).
5 Barnard, *A new anatomy of Ireland*, p. 67.
6 Cronin, *Robert French of Monivea*, pp 25–41.
7 M.D.C. Bolton, *Headfort House* (Kells, 1999), p. 18.